The Ultimate Backseat Book

kids' road atlas

Contents

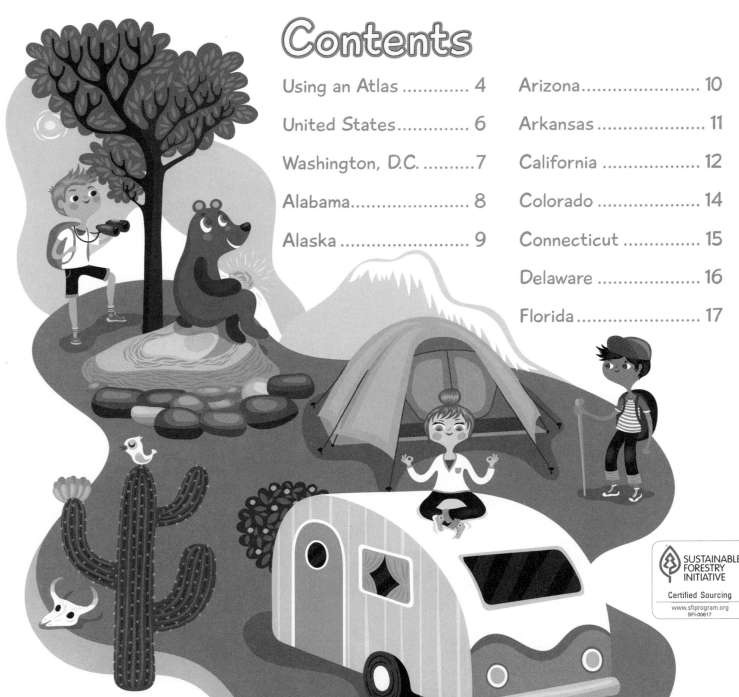

SUSTAINABLE
FORESTRY
INITIATIVE

Certified Sourcing

www.sfiprogram.org
SFI-00617

Using an Atlas...

Adventure or Mystery?

Is map reading an adventure or a mystery? It's only a mystery if you haven't uncovered the clues and codes. The information below will help you unlock the mystery and get started on the adventure. Solve the clues and use the numbered letters to fill in the secret message. For some of the clues you'll need to use the legend, scale, and coordinates, but for others you'll have to do a bit more detective work. Take a closer look at the maps for familiar cities, bordering states, and other details to help you find the answers. Good luck!

Map Legend

Road symbols

▬▬	Freeway or Tollway
───	Highway
(40)	Interstate highway
(65)	U.S. highway
[40]	Canadian highways
(1)	Mexican highway
(15)(9)	State or provincial highways

City symbols

★	National capital
★	State capital
●	City or town

Map symbols

0 10 mi. / 0 10 km.	Map Scale
(N)	North Arrow

Other symbols

■	Point of interest
▲	Mountain peak
	Park area
	Lake or reservoir
───	River or canal
▬▬	State boundary

Legend

The legend, or map key, is a description of the symbols and lines on the map. Use the legend at the left for all of the maps in *Kids' Road Atlas*.

Clue #1: What National Park (N.P.) is at the southernmost section of the map at the right?

___ ___ ___ ___ ___ ___ ___ ___ ___ ___ N.P.
          1   2

Clue #2: In what state will you find this park?

___ ___ ___ ___ ___ ___ ___
      3   4

Scale

Maps come in all sizes. Some show the whole world and others show only a small neighborhood. The map scale tells you how space on a map equals distance on the earth. Scale is used to measure distances between places on a map. Measure the length of the distance from place to place on the map and then use the scale to find out how many miles or kilometers that is. The maps in Kids' Road Atlas are not all at the same scale, so be sure to look at the scale on each map to measure distance correctly.

Clue #3: On the map at the right, what "mile-high" city is approximately 30 miles southeast of Boulder on Interstate 25?

___ ___
5   6

Clue #4: In what state will you find these two cities?

___ ___
7   8

Coordinates

A coordinate is a letter–number combination that helps you find places on a map. To locate a city, look in the index to find the coordinate for that city. If, for example, the coordinate for the city is B–5, look down the right or left edge of the map for the letter B and draw an imaginary line across the map. Then, look across the top or bottom of the map for the number 5 and draw an imaginary line down or up until it meets the imaginary line drawn from the letter B. The city will be inside the area around this point. For each map in the *Kids' Road Atlas* there is an orange coordinate border with letters and numbers.

Clue #5: What coastal city on the map below is at coordinate H–5? Hint: There are several, so make sure you pick the one that fits in the blanks.

___ ___ ___   ___   ___
9 10 11   12   13

Clue #6: In what state is this city located?

___ ___
14   15

Clue #7: You'll find this Mexican city at coordinate I–5.

___ ___ ___
16   17   18

Have you solved all the clues? Congratulations! Use the letters from the numbered spaces in your answers to figure out this secret message:

___ ___ ___   ___ ___ ___ ___ ___ ___ ___ ___ ___
16 13 5   18 4 6 5 15 16 17 8 5

___ ___ ___ ___ ___ ___   ___ ___ ___ ___   ___   ___ ___ ___ ___
12 5 1 3 15 2   10 3 16 13   18   16 17 8 15

___ ___   ___ ___ ___   ___ ___ ___ ___ !
7 14   16 13 5   11 18 1 5

United States

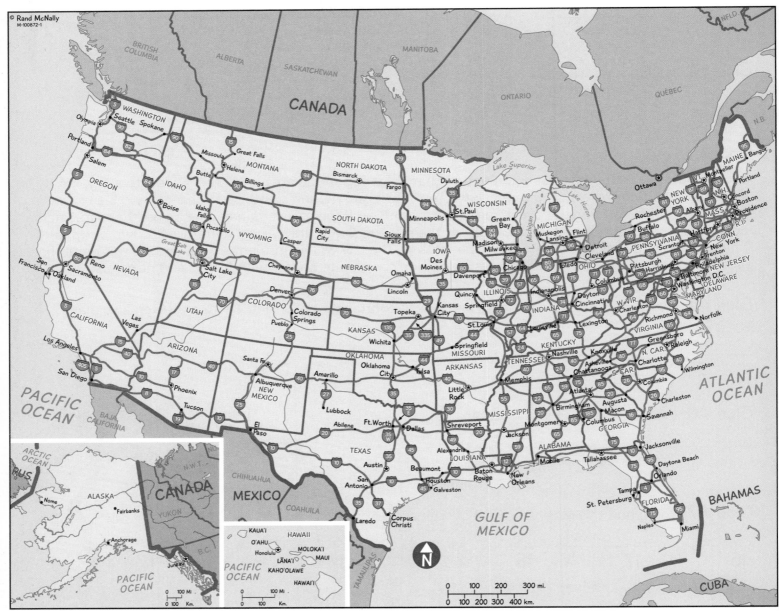

Keep it Brief

Each state has a two-letter abbreviation. On the next page, write the abbreviation for each state in the blanks provided. Remember that the two-letter abbreviation should be written in capital letters. Hint: Check out the state names in the red bar at the top of the pages in this book. The two letters of the abbreviation are the two capital letters in the name.

1. _____ Alabama
2. _____ Alaska
3. _____ Arizona
4. _____ Arkansas
5. _____ California
6. _____ Colorado
7. _____ Connecticut
8. _____ Delaware
9. _____ Florida
10. _____ Georgia
11. _____ Hawaii
12. _____ Idaho
13. _____ Illinois
14. _____ Indiana
15. _____ Iowa
16. _____ Kansas
17. _____ Kentucky

18. _____ Louisiana
19. _____ Maine
20. _____ Maryland
21. _____ Massachusetts
22. _____ Michigan
23. _____ Minnesota
24. _____ Mississippi
25. _____ Missouri
26. _____ Montana
27. _____ Nebraska
28. _____ Nevada
29. _____ New Hampshire
30. _____ New Jersey
31. _____ New Mexico
32. _____ New York
33. _____ North Carolina
34. _____ North Dakota

35. _____ Ohio
36. _____ Oklahoma
37. _____ Oregon
38. _____ Pennsylvania
39. _____ Rhode Island
40. _____ South Carolina
41. _____ South Dakota
42. _____ Tennessee
43. _____ Texas
44. _____ Utah
45. _____ Vermont
46. _____ Virginia
47. _____ Washington
48. _____ West Virginia
49. _____ Wisconsin
50. _____ Wyoming

ALabama

Southern pine | Camellia | Yellowhammer

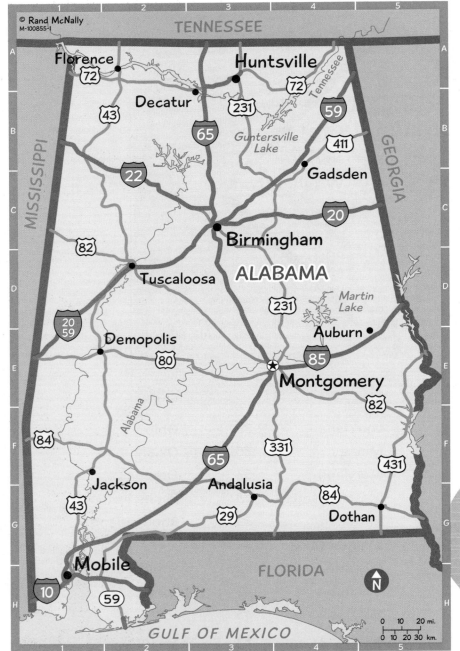

© Rand McNally
M-100855-1

TENNESSEE

Florence 72

Huntsville 72

Decatur

231

43

65

59

411

Guntersville Lake

22

Gadsden

20

Birmingham

82

ALABAMA

Tuscaloosa

MISSISSIPPI

GEORGIA

231

Martin Lake

20 59

Demopolis

80

Auburn

85

Montgomery

Alabama

82

84

331

65

431

Jackson

Andalusia

84

43

29

Dothan

Mobile

FLORIDA

10

59

N

GULF OF MEXICO

0 10 20 mi.
0 10 20 30 km.

BLAST OFF!

Use the code to discover where the Space and Rocket Center is located. Write the correct letters in the blanks at the bottom of the page.

8

AlasKa

Sitka spruce | Forget-me-not | Willow ptarmigan

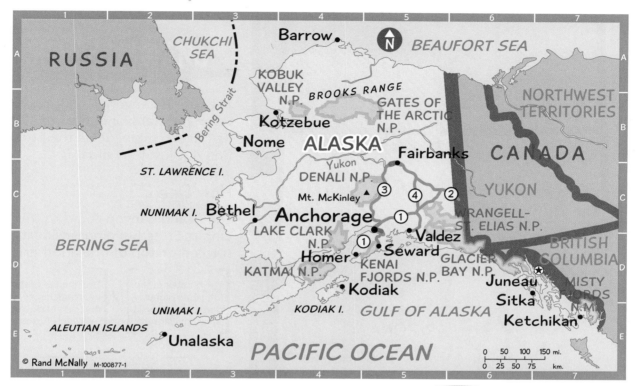

RUSSIA

CHUKCHI SEA

Barrow

BEAUFORT SEA

KOBUK VALLEY N.P.

BROOKS RANGE

GATES OF THE ARCTIC N.P.

NORTHWEST TERRITORIES

Kotzebue

Nome

ALASKA

Fairbanks

CANADA

ST. LAWRENCE I.

Yukon

DENALI N.P.

Mt. McKinley ▲ ③ ④ ②

YUKON

NUNIMAK I.

Bethel

Anchorage

LAKE CLARK N.P.

① ①

Valdez

Seward

WRANGELL-ST. ELIAS N.P.

BRITISH COLUMBIA

BERING SEA

Homer

KATMAI N.P.

KENAI FJORDS N.P.

GLACIER BAY N.P.

Juneau

Sitka

MISTY FJORDS N.M.

Kodiak

UNIMAK I.

KODIAK I.

GULF OF ALASKA

Ketchikan

ALEUTIAN ISLANDS

Unalaska

PACIFIC OCEAN

0 50 100 150 mi.
0 25 50 75 km.

© Rand McNally M-100877-1

DiSCOVeriNG ALaSKa

Circle the Alaska words in the grid.

ANCHORAGE
BALD EAGLE
DOG SLED RACE
ESKIMO
GLACIER
GOLD
GRIZZLY BEAR
IGLOO
JUNEAU
KAYAK

MOOSE
MOUNTAIN
OTTER
SALMON
SNOW
TREE
REINDEER
TUNDRA
WATERFALL
WHALE

K	L	L	A	F	R	E	T	A	W	M	O
B	A	L	D	E	A	G	L	E	S	O	A
S	U	Y	L	T	R	E	E	N	L	O	N
R	A	E	A	T	D	L	O	G	O	S	C
E	E	L	S	K	N	W	I	L	M	E	H
E	N	G	M	O	U	N	T	A	I	N	O
D	U	O	T	O	T	O	A	C	K	L	R
N	J	A	S	K	N	T	A	I	S	S	A
I	O	O	W	H	A	L	E	E	E	N	G
E	D	O	G	S	L	E	D	R	A	C	E
R	A	E	B	Y	L	Z	Z	I	R	G	X

AriZona

Palo verde

Saguaro cactus blossom

Cactus wren

NEVADA
UTAH
COLORADO
NEW MEXICO
CALIFORNIA
MEXICO
SONORA

Lake Mead
Hoover Dam
LAKE MEAD N.R.A.
Kingman
Prescott
Yuma
Gulf of California

Page
Lake Powell
Colorado
GRAND CANYON N.P.
Flagstaff
PETRIFIED FOREST N.P.
ARIZONA
Springerville
Phoenix
Globe
Gila
SAGUARO N.P.
Tucson
Nogales
Douglas

15 160 191 89 40 89 93 40 17 60 60 10 191 70 95 8 85 10 10 19 191

© Rand McNally
M-100856-1

MIGHTY GRAND

The Grand Canyon (C–2) is one of the seven natural wonders of the world. Its size is incredible! Solve the problems to find out just how big it is.

How Deep?

The Grand Canyon could fit this many Empire State Buildings inside its walls, stacked on top of one another!

$$\left[\begin{array}{c}\text{The number of the}\\\text{Interstate highway}\\\text{that runs east-west}\\\text{through Flagstaff}\end{array}\right] \Big/ \left[\begin{array}{c}\text{The number of the}\\\text{Interstate highway}\\\text{that runs east-west}\\\text{through Tuscon}\end{array}\right] =$$

___ = ___ ___

How Long?

The Grand Canyon is this many miles long—almost the same as the width of the state of Utah!

$$\left[\begin{array}{c}\text{The number}\\\text{of the}\\\text{U.S highway}\\\text{that runs}\\\text{down}\\\text{Arizona's}\\\text{eastern}\\\text{border}\end{array}\right] + \left[\begin{array}{c}\text{The number}\\\text{of the}\\\text{state}\\\text{highway}\\\text{that}\\\text{runs from}\\\text{Globe to}\\\text{Springerville}\end{array}\right] - \left[\begin{array}{c}\text{The number}\\\text{of the}\\\text{Interstate}\\\text{highway}\\\text{running}\\\text{west from}\\\text{Phoenix}\end{array}\right] +$$

$$\left[\begin{array}{c}\text{The number of the}\\\text{Interstate highway}\\\text{that runs north}\\\text{from Phoenix}\end{array}\right] + \left[\begin{array}{c}\text{The number of the}\\\text{Interstate highway}\\\text{that runs from}\\\text{south from Tucson}\end{array}\right] =$$

___ ___ ___ ___

=

ARkansas

Pine

Apple blossom

Mockingbird

Road Rally

It's a road rally from Hot Springs (D–3) to where? When you race in a rally you are given a map with your beginning city only. Can you figure out which towns are on the route after Hot Springs? Use the map above to help fill in the blanks on the Road Rally Map.

CAlifornia

Nickname: The Golden State **Capital:** Sacramento

 California redwood

 Golden poppy

 California (valley) quail

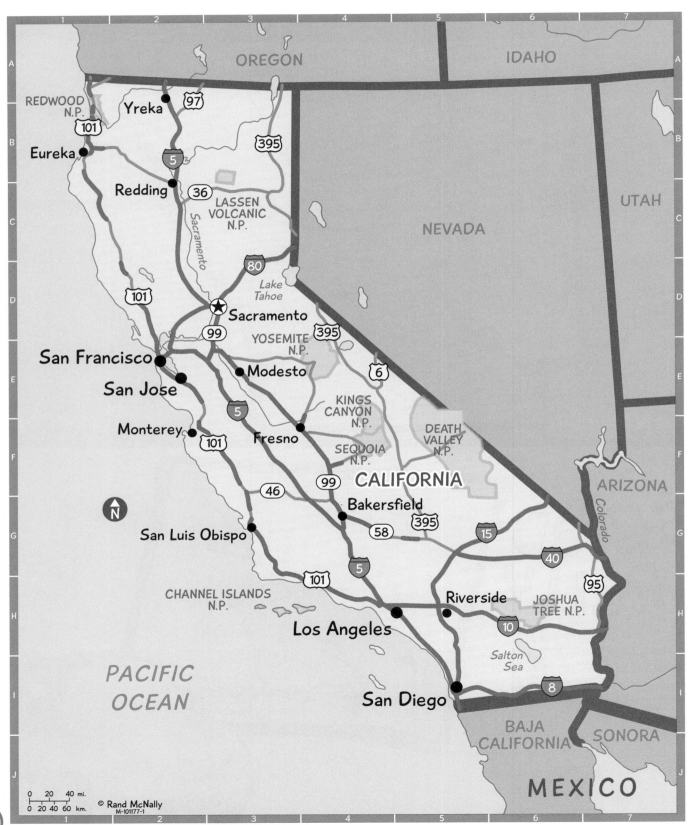

OREGON

IDAHO

REDWOOD N.P.

Yreka 97

Eureka

101

Redding 36

5

395

LASSEN VOLCANIC N.P.

Sacramento

UTAH

NEVADA

80

Lake Tahoe

Sacramento

Sacramento

99

YOSEMITE N.P.

395

San Francisco

Modesto

6

San Jose

101

Monterey

5

KINGS CANYON N.P.

DEATH VALLEY N.P.

Fresno

SEQUOIA N.P.

CALIFORNIA

ARIZONA

99

46

Bakersfield

N

San Luis Obispo

58

395

15

Colorado

101

5

40

95

CHANNEL ISLANDS N.P.

Riverside

JOSHUA TREE N.P.

10

Los Angeles

Salton Sea

PACIFIC OCEAN

San Diego

8

BAJA CALIFORNIA

SONORA

MEXICO

0 20 40 mi.
0 20 40 60 km.

© Rand McNally
M-101177-1

12

Park it here

Look at the map of California for the National Parks that are located at the coordinates listed below. Write the names of the parks in the puzzle. The shaded column will spell out California's state motto, reading from top to bottom.

1. B–1
2. F–4
3. H–6
4. D–3
5. E–4
6. F–5

COlorado

Nickname: The Centennial State | Capital: Denver

Colorado blue spruce | Columbine | Lark bunting

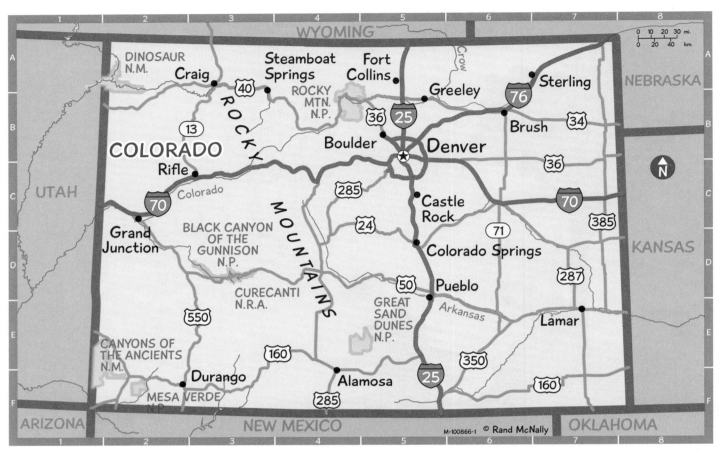

WYOMING

DINOSAUR N.M. · Craig · 40 · Steamboat Springs · Fort Collins · Greeley · 76 · Sterling · NEBRASKA

ROCKY MTN. N.P. · 36 · 25 · Brush · 34

13 · COLORADO · Boulder · Denver · 36

Rifle · Colorado · 285 · Castle Rock · 70 · 385

UTAH · 70 · Grand Junction · BLACK CANYON OF THE GUNNISON N.P. · 24 · 71 · Colorado Springs · KANSAS

MOUNTAINS · CURECANTI N.R.A. · 550 · 50 · Pueblo · Arkansas · 287

GREAT SAND DUNES N.P. · Lamar

CANYONS OF THE ANCIENTS N.M. · 160 · 350

Durango · Alamosa · 25 · 160

MESA VERDE N.P. · 285

ARIZONA · NEW MEXICO · M-100866-1 © Rand McNally · OKLAHOMA

0 10 20 30 mi.
0 20 40 km.

N

THE NAME GAME

B-6

A lot of places in Colorado are named after objects. Look at the pictures below. Can you find the places named after them? Their coordinates are given in parentheses.

B-5 _____

C-3 _____

C-5 _____ +

A-3 + _____

A-2 _____ National Monument

River A-6 _____

14

ConnecTicut

Nickname : The Constitution State

Capital : Hartford

White oak | Mountain laurel | American robin

MASSACHUSETTS

44
202
91
84
Putnam
395

7

8

Hartford

CONNECTICUT

RHODE ISLAND

NEW YORK

New Milford

Waterbury

2

Norwich

84

15

Connecticut

9

395

95

Danbury

8

New London

Mystic Aquarium

7

91

N

New Haven

15

95

Bridgeport

Long Island Sound

Stamford

© Rand McNally
M-101142-1

NEW YORK

ATLANTIC OCEAN

Sea Creature

Color the shapes that contain vowels to find out what's at the Mystic Aquarium (D–5).

15

DElaware

American holly | Peach blossom | Blue hen chicken

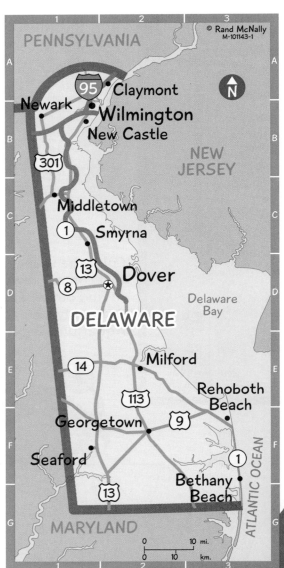

Delaware is well-known for its maritime history. Can you spot the correct reflection for this ship?

SHip Shape

FLorida

Sabal palm | Orange blossom | Mockingbird

SiT FOR a SpeLL

The Florida beach below shows objects that can be grouped into pairs in which the letters of one thing can be rearranged to spell another. For example, HORSE and SHORE are a pair because they contain the same letters. Rearrange the letters in the words given to make other pairs.

ALABAMA
GEORGIA
Pensacola
Tallahassee
Panama City
Jacksonville
St. Augustine
ATLANTIC OCEAN
Ocala
Daytona Beach
Orlando
Tampa
St. Petersburg
FLORIDA
FLORIDA'S TPK.
Port St. Lucie
Lake Okeechobee
Ft. Myers
Fort Lauderdale
GULF OF MEXICO
EVERGLADES N.P.
Miami
Biscayne National Park
DRY TORTUGAS N.P.
Key West

© Rand McNally
M-100857-1

HORSE _____SHORE_____   MELON _____

OCEAN _____   TEN _____

PALM _____   SHOE _____

PEARS _____   BEARD _____

(17)

GeorgiA

Live oak

Cherokee rose

Brown thrasher

Peanuts are an important crop in Georgia. Can you find your way through the peanut maze?

FiNiSH

18

Hawaii

Nickname: The Aloha State | Capital: Honolulu

Kukui (candlenut)

Yellow hibiscus

Nene (Hawaiian goose)

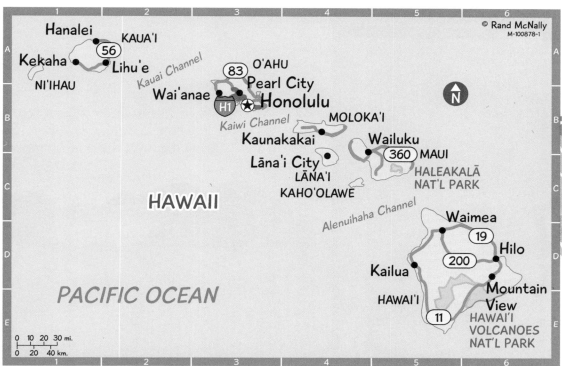

© Rand McNally
M-100878-1

Map labels:
- Hanalei
- KAUA'I
- Kekaha
- 56
- Lihu'e
- NI'IHAU
- Kauai Channel
- O'AHU
- 83
- Pearl City
- Wai'anae
- Honolulu
- H1
- Kaiwi Channel
- MOLOKA'I
- Kaunakakai
- Wailuku
- Lāna'i City
- 360
- MAUI
- LĀNA'I
- HALEAKALĀ NAT'L PARK
- KAHO'OLAWE
- HAWAII
- Alenuihaha Channel
- Waimea
- 19
- Hilo
- 200
- Kailua
- Mountain View
- HAWAI'I
- 11
- HAWAI'I VOLCANOES NAT'L PARK
- PACIFIC OCEAN
- N

Scale: 0 10 20 30 mi. / 0 20 40 km.

active Hawaii

Connect the dots to find out what Kilauea is. Kilauea is in the National Park at coordinate E–6.

IDaho

Nickname : **The Gem State**

Capital : **Boise**

Western white pine | Syringa (mock orange) | Mountain bluebird

BRITISH COLUMBIA   CANADA   ALBERTA

WATERTON-GLACIER INT'L PEACE PARK

Bonners Ferry

WASHINGTON

Coeur d'Alene
90
95

MONTANA

Moscow

Lewiston
12

ROCKY MOUNTAINS

HELLS CANYON N.R.A.

Salmon

Salmon
93

IDAHO

95

55

SAWTOOTH N.R.A.

93

YELLOWSTONE N.P.

15   20

Boise
★

Nampa

Mountain Home

Snake

75

CRATERS OF THE MOON N.M. & PRES.

26

Idaho Falls

84

Pocatello

86

30

Twin Falls
93

Shoshone Falls

84

15

OREGON

NEVADA   UTAH

0 10 20 30 mi.
0 20 40 km.

© Rand McNally
M-101162-1

Spuds Aplenty

Idaho is known for growing lots of potatoes. Find 5 potatoes and 5 french fries hidden in this picture of Shoshone Falls (G-3), the "Niagara Falls of the West."

ILLinois

White oak | Native violet | Cardinal

tour of illinois

Follow the directions for a tour of Illinois. Write the names of the cities you visit as you go.

1. _____
A place to say "Bonjour." (E–5)

2. _____
A place for Santa Claus and Abraham Lincoln. (D–2)

3. _____
A place to have lunch. (B–4)

4. _____
A place to avoid. (B–3)

5. _____
A place to have an average time. (C–4)

6. _____
A place where a poor speller could celebrate. (D–4)

21

INdiana

Nickname: The Hoosier State | **Capital:** Indianapolis

Tulip tree | Peony | Cardinal

A Day at the Races

In the Indy 500 car race it can be hard to tell who is winning. Some cars can be laps ahead of the others. Use the clues below to figure out which car is winning and which cars are coming in 2nd and 3rd.

1. None of the odd numbered cars finished in the top three.

2. The gray car didn't finish in the top three.

3. The yellow car didn't win.

4. The brown car didn't finish in the top three.

5. The red car came in right behind the orange car.

1st_____

2nd_____

3rd_____

© Rand McNally M-100867-1

Oak | Wild rose | Eastern goldfinch

MINNESOTA

S.D.

71

18

75

Mason City

35

218

18

WISCONSIN

Sioux City

Waterloo

Dubuque

20

20

380

151

61

IOWA

Ames

30

Cedar Rapids

30

Bettendorf

Des Moines

80

Iowa City

Davenport

NEBRASKA

80

Council Bluffs

71

34

218

ILLINOIS

61

29

34

Burlington

35

MISSOURI

© Rand McNally
M-100890-1

Missouri

Des Moines

Mississippi

FaRm juMBLe

The names of 7 farm animals are mixed up below. Unscramble them and write the correct names in the boxes. The shaded letters, reading from top to bottom, will spell out the name of something that is made in Iowa. More of this product is made in Sioux City than in any other place in the world!

1. GIP
2. TROOSER
3. HEEPS
4. CWO
5. TOGA
6. RHOSE
7. NECKHIC

1.
2.
3.
4.
5.
6.
7.

24

KanSas

Nickname: The Sunflower State | Capital: Topeka

Cottonwood | Native sunflower | Western meadowlark

Dodge City, Kansas, was a famous town in the Old West. Circle what doesn't belong in this Old West scene.

OLD WEST?

25

KentuckY

Nickname: **The Bluegrass State** | Capital: **Frankfort**

Tulip poplar | Goldenrod | Cardinal

ILLINOIS
INDIANA
OHIO
Covington
75
68
Louisville
Frankfort
WEST VIRGINIA
64
Lawrenceburg
Lexington
65
COMBS MTN. PKWY.
23
Ohio
BLUE GRASS PKWY.
Owensboro
60
Richmond
BREATHITT PENNYRILE
NATCHER PKWY.
Danville
KENTUCKY
80
Pikeville
Madisonville
27
Paducah
MISSOURI
Bowling Green
MAMMOTH CAVE N.P.
ROGERS PKWY.
24
London
VIRGINIA
Cumberland
51
NUNN CUMBERLAND PKWY.
68
75
Russellville
90
Williamsburg
LAND BETWEEN THE LAKES N.R.A.
Lake Barkley
BIG SOUTH FORK NAT'L R. & REC. AREA
Kentucky Lake
TENNESSEE
NORTH CAROLINA
© Rand McNally
M-100880-1

BOY Oh BOY!

The name "Ken" can be found in the first three letters of Kentucky. How many boys' names can you find hidden in the cities on the map of Kentucky?

Hint: All of the names do not occur at the beginning of the city names.

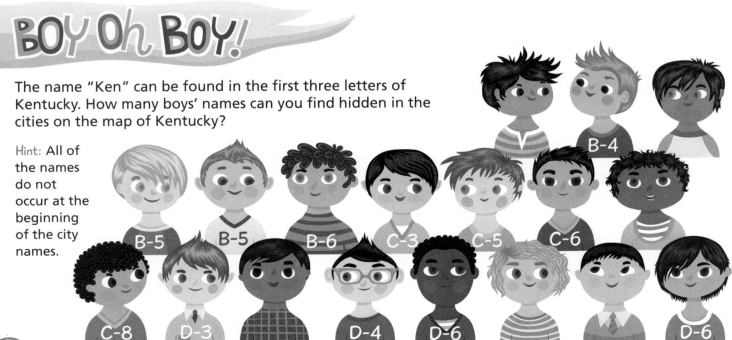

B-4

B-5 B-5 B-6 C-3 C-5 C-6

C-8 D-3 D-4 D-6 D-6

LouisiAna

Nickname: The Pelican State | **Capital:** Baton Rouge

Bald cypress | Magnolia | Eastern brown pelican

ARKANSAS

Caddo L. · Shreveport · 20 · Monroe

L. Bistineau

LOUISIANA

Ouachita · 65

165

Red

Catahoula L.

Toledo Bend Res. · 49

171

TEXAS

Sabine

Atchafalaya

Baton Rouge · 55

Lake Charles · 190 · Pearl · 12

10 · Lafayette · Lake Pontchartrain

Calcasieu L. · Grand L. · White L. · 10 · Metarie · Lake Borgne · New Orleans

90 · Houma · 23

Mississippi

GULF OF MEXICO · Atchafalaya Bay

© Rand McNally
M-100892-1

MISSISSIPPI

ALABAMA

N

BiG RiVErS

Can you fit the names of these Louisiana rivers, bayous, and lakes into the grid? One of the lake names is in the puzzle to get you started.
Hint: Counting the number of letters in the words and using the color code will help.

RIVERS: Mississippi, Red, Ouachita, Sabine, Pearl, Atchafalaya, Black

BAYOUS: Teche, Lafourche, Macon, Boeuf, Dorcheat, D'Arbonne

LAKES: Pontchartrain, Calcasieu, White, Borgne, Caddo, Bistineau, Toledo Bend Reservoir, Grand, Catahoula

G
R
A
N
D

MainE

White pine

White pine
cone & tassel

Chickadee

CANADA

QUÉBEC

St. John

Chamberlain
Lake

11

Presque Isle

1

NEW BRUNSWICK

MAINE

Houlton

Moosehead
Lake

95

201

Dover-
Foxcraft

6

Lincoln

150

Eastport

Farmington

2

Bangor

1

Augusta

Waterville

3

3

Bar Harbor

26

Auburn

1

ACADIA
NATIONAL
PARK

295

95

Brunswick

202

Portland

Biddeford

ATLANTIC
OCEAN

N.H.

© Rand McNally
M-100879-1

0   10   20   30 mi.
0   10   20   30   40 km.

LiGHtS OUt!

Help the lighthouse keeper
get to the top to warn the ships.

MarylanD

Nickname: The Old Line State | Capital: Annapolis

White oak | Black-eyed susan | Baltimore oriole

© Rand McNally
M-100894-1

PENNSYLVANIA

Cumberland · 68
219
WEST VIRGINIA
Hagerstown ·
Frederick
70
83 1 95
NEW JERSEY
Baltimore
Fort McHenry N.M.
301
Annapolis ★ · Easton
DELAWARE
Washington ·
301
50
VIRGINIA
MARYLAND
Salisbury
13 113
Ocean City
Chesapeake Bay
ASSATEAGUE I. NAT'L SEASHORE
ATLANTIC OCEAN

N

0 10 20 30 mi.
0 10 20 30 40 km.

1. Oh! Say can you see, by the dawn's early light,
2. what so proudly we hailed at the twilight's last gleaming?
3. Whose broad stripes and bright stars through the perilous fight,
4. o'er the ramparts we watched were so gallantly streaming?
5. And the rockets' red glare,
6. the bombs bursting in air
7. gave proof through the night
8. that our flag was still there.
9. Oh! Say does that star-spangled banner yet wave
10. o'er the land of the free and the home of the brave?

Use the example at the right to understand the code. The letter G is in line number 1, word number 10, and letter number 3.

FLaG SonG

$$\frac{G}{}$$
line 1
word 10
letter 3

Francis Scott Key wrote the National Anthem in Maryland during the Battle of Baltimore in the War of 1812. Solve the code to find out where he was when he wrote these famous words.

9	7	8	2	3	5	2	4	4	2	4	7	5	5
1	4	4	1	6	1	3	3	9	8	1	5	5	4
2	3	1	3	1	1	1	1	7	9	1	1	5	1

10	10	8	6	1	3	4	6	9	1	2	3	4	7
9	3	3	2	9	3	3	4	2	7	2	10	9	2
2	3	3	1	3	4	7	1	1	2	1	4	7	1

American elm | Mayflower | Black-capped chickadee

Bay Staters

Many famous people were born in or lived in Massachusetts. The names of fifteen of them are hidden in the word search on the next page. (Only the last names are hidden.)

(JOHN) ADAMS
(LOUISA MAY) ALCOTT
(SUSAN B.) ANTHONY
(CLARA) BARTON
(EMILY) DICKINSON

(W.E.B.) DUBOIS
(RALPH WALDO) EMERSON
(BENJAMIN) FRANKLIN
(JOHN) HANCOCK
(OLIVER WENDELL) HOLMES

(WINSLOW) HOMER
(JOHN F.) KENNEDY
(EDGAR ALLAN) POE
(PAUL) REVERE
(NORMAN) ROCKWELL

```
A D R L P O E
E X I H O L M E S
F A N C D E C E R E
G R R K A H M K R A
M B A I R E E E W H
L S L N R E V H A E N
K E I S K E M N N O L A
N E O O R L C O T R L L
N N N B O I R H C Y
D N C U A N O A
V K E B D T N I D
T H O D T R Y E A
A D A M S Y U
```

MIchigan

White pine

Apple blossom

Robin

ISLE ROYALE N.P.
Copper Harbor
LAKE SUPERIOR
CANADA
ONTARIO
PICTURED ROCKS NAT'L LAKESHORE
MINN.
Ironwood
2
Marquette
141
Sault Ste. Marie
75
WIS.
Iron Mtn.
2
Escanaba
Mackinaw City
SLEEPING BEAR SAND DUNES NAT'L LAKESHORE
Alpena
Menominee
Traverse City
MICHIGAN
23
LAKE HURON
31
Ludington
75
10
Bay City
131
127
Saginaw
Port Huron
Muskegon
Grand Rapids
Flint
69
LAKE MICHIGAN
Lansing ★
96
St. Joseph
94
Detroit
LAKE ERIE
INDIANA
OHIO

© Rand McNally
M-100870-1

You are the inspector for this line of new cars in Detroit, the "Motor City." Circle the six differences between the standard and the other cars.

Standard

Quality Control

MiNnesota

Norway pine

Pink-and-white lady's slipper

Common loon

Minnesota is called the land of 10,000 lakes. Use the coordinates and clues to find a few of these lakes.

© Rand McNally
M-100896-1

ACROSS
3. E–3; unscramble LIMEL
4. C–4; rhymes with 1,000,000
6. D–3; hope not to find these in the lake

DOWN
1. C–2; above and rosy
2. D–3; 14 letters in this name
5. D–2; L. and unscramble ASTICA
6. C–2; below and rosy

33

MiSsissippi

Magnolia | Magnolia | Mockingbird

© Rand McNally
M-100897-1

TENNESSEE

ARKANSAS

72
Corinth
78
45
278
Tupelo
Clarksdale
MISSISSIPPI
82
Columbus
82
Greenville
Winona
25
45
61
49
Jackson
Meridian
20
Vicksburg
Pearl
ALABAMA
55
84
Natchez
98
61
Hattiesburg
98
59
49
63
LOUISIANA
Biloxi
10
Gulfport
GULF ISLANDS
NAT'L SEASHORE
GULF OF MEXICO

Mississippi

N

plenty OF p's

Can you find 20 things that start with "P" in this scene on the Mississippi River?

MissOuri

Nickname: The Show Me State | Capital: Jefferson City

Flowering dogwood | Hawthorn blossom | Bluebird

MISSOURI

NEBRASKA · IOWA · ILLINOIS · INDIANA
KANSAS · KENTUCKY · TENNESSEE · ARKANSAS · OKLAHOMA

St. Joseph · Hannibal · Kansas City · Columbia · St. Louis · Jefferson City · Harry S. Truman Res. · Lake of the Ozarks · Missouri · Mississippi · OZARK NAT'L SCENIC RIVERWAY · Springfield · Joplin · Cape Girardeau · Branson

29 · 71 · 136 · 65 · 63 · 35 · 36 · 54 · 70 · 49 · 44 · 8 · 54 · 65 · 63 · 60 · 67 · 49 · 63 · 60 · 55

© Rand McNally
M-100882-1

BORDER patrol

Eight states share borders with Missouri. Can you fit the names of the bordering states into the puzzle?

N

A

MonTana

Nickname: The Treasure State | Capital: Helena

Ponderosa pine | Bitterroot | Western meadowlark

CANADA

B.C. ALBERTA | SASKATCHEWAN

WATERTON-GLACIER INT'L PEACE PK.

Kalispell

Shelby

Havre

Wolf Point

Flathead Lake

UPPER MISSOURI RIVER BREAKS N.M.

Fort Peck Lake

Missouri

ROCKY

Great Falls

MONTANA

Glendive

Missoula

Helena

Miles City

MOUNTAINS

Yellowstone

Butte

Billings

N

Bozeman

BIGHORN CANYON N.R.A.

IDAHO

Dillon

YELLOWSTONE N.P.

WYOMING

N. DAKOTA

S. DAKOTA

© Rand McNally
M-100898-1

After a morning of boarding at Big Sky Resort, this snowboarder went in for lunch. When he came out, he couldn't remember where he had put his snowboard. Using the clues that he recalls, help him find his board.

1. His snowboard isn't next to a pair of skis.
2. His snowboard is not blue.
3. His snowboard is next to a blue snowboard.

NEbraska

Cottonwood | Goldenrod | Western meadowlark

thrown for a loop

The cowboy tradition is alive and kicking in Nebraska. Here, a few cowboys have been practicing their roping tricks. Some of the ropes lying on the ground will form knots when both ends are pulled. Can you tell which ones?

NeVada

Single-leaf piñon | Sagebrush | Mountain bluebird

OREGON

IDAHO

McDermitt

140 · 95

93

223

Winnemucca

80

Elko

Spring Creek

West Wendover

UTAH

Pyramid Lake

80

305

278

Sparks

Fallon

50

50

Reno

Ely

Carson City

NEVADA

Lake Tahoe

95

376

6

GREAT BASIN N.P.

93

Tonopah

CALIFORNIA

DEATH VALLEY N.P.

95

Mesquite

15

LAKE MEAD N.R.A.

Las Vegas

Henderson

ARIZONA

Colorado

95

© Rand McNally
M-100900-1

0 10 20 30 mi.
0   20   40 km.

BRiGHt LiGHtS, WHat CitY?

Hidden within the colorful lights is the answer to the riddle. All you have to do is fill in the bulbs marked with an "X."

Riddle: What city has the highest electric bills in America?

New Hampshire

White birch | Purple lilac | Purple finch

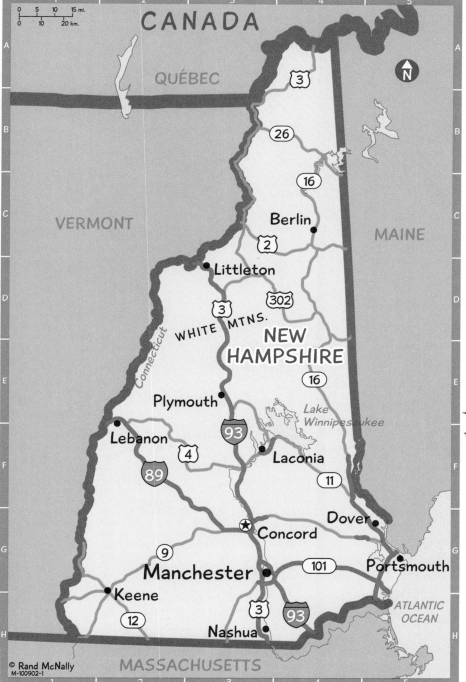

CANADA

QUÉBEC

VERMONT

MAINE

3

26

16

Berlin

2

Littleton

302

3

WHITE MTNS.

NEW HAMPSHIRE

16

Plymouth

93

Lebanon

4

Laconia

89

11

Dover

Concord

9

101

Portsmouth

Manchester

Keene

3   93

12

Nashua

ATLANTIC OCEAN

MASSACHUSETTS

Connecticut

Lake Winnipesaukee

© Rand McNally
M-100902-1

UNDER a SpeLL

How many things can you find in this scene that can only be spelled using letters found in the words NEW HAMPSHIRE?

New Jersey

Nickname: The Garden State
Capital: Trenton

Red oak | Purple violet | Eastern goldfinch

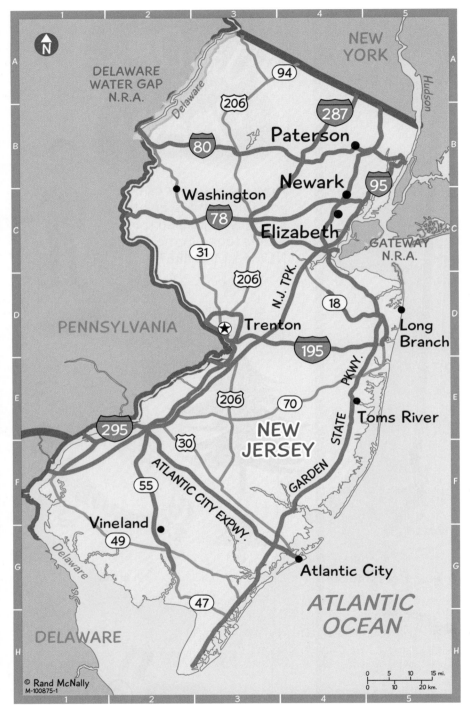

DELAWARE WATER GAP N.R.A.

NEW YORK

Delaware

94
206
287

Paterson

80

Newark

95

Washington

78

Elizabeth

GATEWAY N.R.A.

31

206

N.J. TPK.

18

Trenton

Long Branch

195

206

70

Toms River

295

NEW JERSEY

STATE PKWY.

GARDEN

30

ATLANTIC CITY EXPWY.

55

Vineland

49

Atlantic City

47

DELAWARE

ATLANTIC OCEAN

PENNSYLVANIA

Hudson

© Rand McNally
M-100875-1

0 5 10 15 mi.
0 10 20 km.

SHORE THINGS

Connect the dots to see what's on this New Jersey beach.

40

New Mexico

Nickname: Land of Enchantment
Capital: Santa Fe

Piñon pine | Yucca | Roadrunner

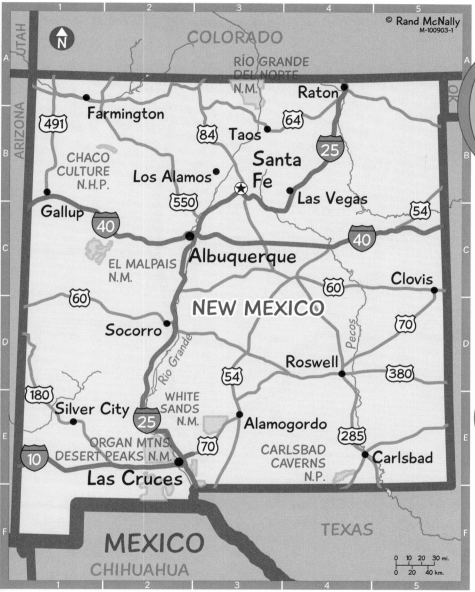

© Rand McNally
M-100903-1

COLORADO

UTAH

ARIZONA

N

RÍO GRANDE DEL NORTE N.M.

491 Farmington

Raton

64

84 Taos

25

Santa Fe

CHACO CULTURE N.H.P.

Los Alamos

550

Las Vegas

54

Gallup

40

Albuquerque

40

EL MALPAIS N.M.

Clovis

60

NEW MEXICO

60

70

Socorro

Rio Grande

Pecos

Roswell

380

180

54

Silver City

25

WHITE SANDS N.M.

Alamogordo

285

10

ORGAN MTNS. DESERT PEAKS N.M.

70

Carlsbad

Las Cruces

CARLSBAD CAVERNS N.P.

TEXAS

MEXICO

CHIHUAHUA

OKLAHOMA

0 10 20 30 mi.
0   20   40 km.

The Hot Air Balloon Festival in Albuquerque is the most photographed event of its kind in the world! New Mexico is famous for another hot thing—its Southwestern food. Can you find the 10 chili peppers hiding in this scene?

HOT tiME

New York

Sugar maple | Rose | Red-breasted bluebird

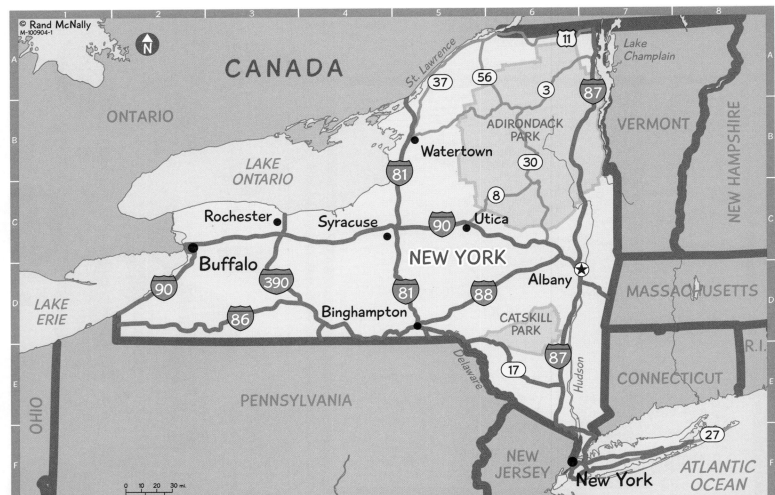

© Rand McNally
M-100904-1

CANADA

ONTARIO

LAKE ONTARIO

Watertown

ADIRONDACK PARK

Lake Champlain

VERMONT

NEW HAMPSHIRE

Rochester

Syracuse

Utica

Buffalo

NEW YORK

Albany

MASSACHUSETTS

LAKE ERIE

Binghampton

CATSKILL PARK

R.I.

OHIO

PENNSYLVANIA

Delaware

Hudson

CONNECTICUT

NEW JERSEY

New York

ATLANTIC OCEAN

0 10 20 30 mi.
0 20 40 km.

PROBLEMS at the PARK

The state of New York has many beautiful parks, but there seems to be something strange going on in this one. Can you spot 10 things wrong in the park?

MAIL MAIL

North Carolina

Nickname: The Tar Heel State

Capital: Raleigh

Pine | Dogwood | Cardinal

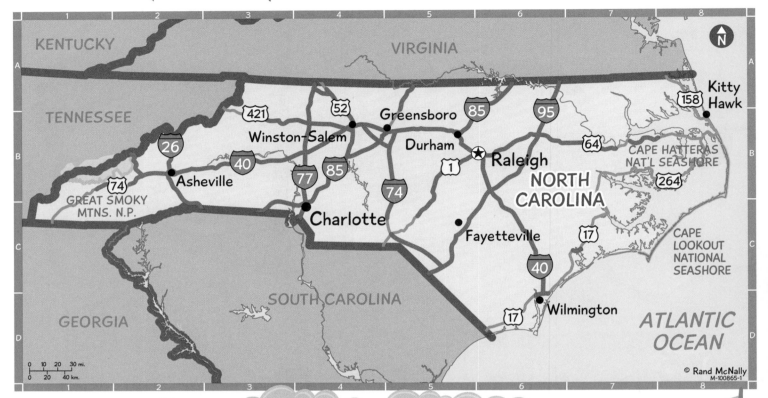

KENTUCKY

VIRGINIA

TENNESSEE

421 52 Greensboro 85 95 Kitty Hawk 158

Winston-Salem Durham 64 CAPE HATTERAS NAT'L SEASHORE

26 40 77 85 1 Raleigh 264

74 Asheville NORTH CAROLINA

74 Charlotte Fayetteville 17

GREAT SMOKY MTNS. N.P. 40

SOUTH CAROLINA CAPE LOOKOUT NATIONAL SEASHORE

GEORGIA 17 Wilmington

ATLANTIC OCEAN

0 10 20 30 mi.
0 20 40 km.

© Rand McNally
M-100865-1

First in Flight

4

The beach community of Kitty Hawk (B-8) was the site of the Wright brothers' first airplane flight. Try to find 26 things that start with "F" in this beach scene.

44

North Dakota

American elm | Wild prairie rose | Western meadowlark

Secret Cities

Figure out the names of six North Dakota cities using the word puzzles below.

1) + =

_____

2) GRRR + and + =

_____

3) V + + =

_____

4) + =

_____

5) + - C + L =

_____

6) + ing + =

_____

OHio

Buckeye | Scarlet carnation | Cardinal

MICHIGAN

CANADA

ONTARIO

LAKE ERIE

90

PENNSYLVANIA

INDIANA

Toledo

80 90

Cleveland

CUYAHOGA VALLEY N.P.

Youngstown

Findlay

Ashland

71

Akron

Lima

30

Mansfield

Canton

30

33

OHIO

77

75

127

Columbus

Newark

Cambridge

70

Springfield

70

Dayton

Fairborn

Whitehall

Oxford

71

33

Logan

Ohio

Middletown

35

Chillicothe

Athens

Cincinnati

50

23

Portsmouth

WEST VIRGINIA

KENTUCKY

0 10 20 30 mi.
0 10 20 30 40 km.

© Rand McNally
M-100906-1

SpLit Cities

The names of many cities in Ohio can be split into two smaller words. For example, DAY and TON go together to form DAYTON. Match the words in column A with the words in column B to spell 12 Ohio cities. All of the cities are listed on the map.

Column A	Column B
FIND	LAND
NEW	MOUTH
ASH	FIELD
CAN	TOWN
WHITE	ARK
SPRING	TON
LOG	BORN
AT	AN
PORTS	FORD
OX	LAY
FAIR	HALL
MIDDLE	HENS

OKlahoma

Redbud | Mistletoe | Scissor-tailed flycatcher

Scrambled Cities

Unscramble the names of these Oklahoma towns and you'll be OK!

DINE (B-5) _____

BILEAD (E-8) _____

LOWTAN (E-5) _____

WLASSAIL (C-8) _____

LEEKOMUG (C-7) _____

MOUNGY (A-2) _____

USALT (B-7) _____

AMIMI (A-8) _____

SHEENWA (C-6) _____

TALLIWERTS (B-6) _____

ORegon

Douglas fir | Oregon grape | Western meadowlark

© Rand McNally
M-100883-1

WASHINGTON
PACIFIC OCEAN
Astoria
Columbia
Portland
Salem
Corvallis
OREGON DUNES N.R.A.
Eugene
Coos Bay
Roseburg
CAPE BLANCO
CASCADE RANGE
Medford
CASCADE-SISKIYOU N.M.
Klamath Falls
Upper Klamath Lake
CRATER LAKE N.P.
Bend
OREGON
The Dalles
Pendleton
La Grande
HELLS CANYON N.R.A.
John Day
Ontario
IDAHO
Snake
Malheur Lake
Harney Lake
Burns Junction
NEVADA
CALIFORNIA

Dive In

These two tide pools on the Oregon coast are almost exactly alike. Can you spot the nine differences between them?

PennsylvAnia

Nickname: The Keystone State | Capital: Harrisburg

Hemlock | Mountain laurel | Ruffed grouse

LAKE ERIE

Erie

NEW YORK

90

6

Warren

6

6

81

79

219

15

Scranton

84

80

Williamsport

Wilkes-Barre

PENNSYLVANIA

80

Delaware

New Castle

State College

Susquehanna

NEW JERSEY

76

119

22

322

Allentown

78

476

99

Altoona

Harrisburg

70

Pittsburgh

76

81

83

Philadelphia

95

WEST VIRGINIA

MARYLAND

© Rand McNally
M-100859-1

two of a kind

Two of the squares in this Pennsylvania Dutch quilt are exactly the same. Can you find them?

Rhode Island

Red maple | Violet | Rhode Island red

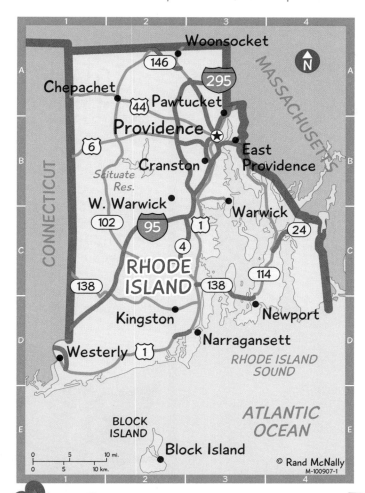

in the RED

People in Rhode Island must like the color red. Their state bird is the Rhode Island red and their state tree is the red maple. Use the clues below to identify words that have RED in them.

1. Stop signal _____

2. Tall California tree _____

3. Colors of the U.S. flag _____

4. Become very angry _____

5. Story about a girl, her grandmother, and a wolf
_____

6. Walking surface for movie stars _____

7. Carrot top _____

WELCOME to RHODE ISLAND

South Carolina

Palmetto

Carolina jessamine

Carolina wren

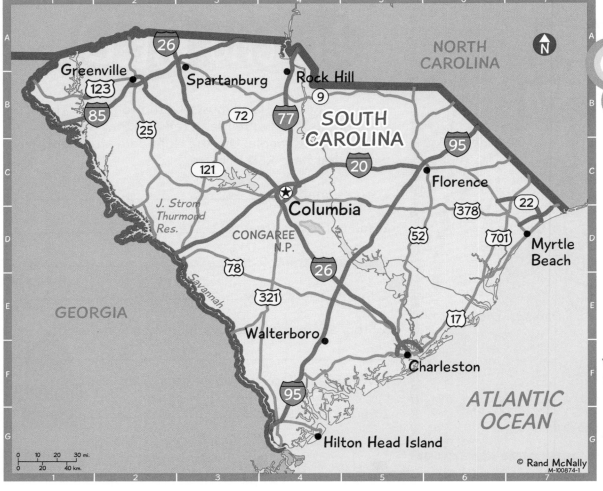

NORTH CAROLINA

SOUTH CAROLINA

Greenville
Spartanburg
Rock Hill
Columbia
Florence
Myrtle Beach
Walterboro
Charleston
Hilton Head Island

J. Strom Thurmond Res.
CONGAREE N.P.
GEORGIA
Savannah
ATLANTIC OCEAN

26 123 85 25 72 77 9 95 20 121 378 22 52 701 78 321 26 17 95

© Rand McNally
M-100874-1

Cotton Critters

Cotton is an important crop in South Carolina. Can you find the pesky boll weevils hidden in the cotton plants? Circle them before they damage the cotton.

(52)

South Dakota

Nickname :
The Mount Rushmore State

Capital :
Pierre

Black Hills spruce | Pasque flower | Chinese ring-necked pheasant

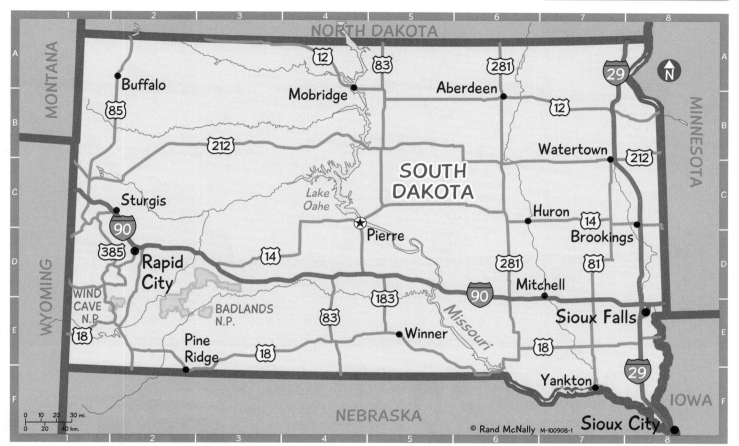

MONTANA

NORTH DAKOTA

Buffalo

85

Mobridge

12

83

Aberdeen

281

12

29

212

Watertown

212

MINNESOTA

Lake Oahe

SOUTH DAKOTA

Sturgis

90

385

Rapid City

WIND CAVE N.P

18

BADLANDS N.P.

Pine Ridge

14

14

Huron

Brookings

14

281

81

Mitchell

90

Sioux Falls

WYOMING

183

83

Winner

18

Missouri

18

Yankton

29

Pierre

IOWA

NEBRASKA

Sioux City

0 10 20 30 mi.
0 20 40 km.

© Rand McNally M-100908-1

Wild & Wooly

The pictures below show the steps in making a sweater—starting with shearing a sheep for wool. However, the pictures are not in the right order. If you write the letters in the corner of the pictures in the order in which they should be placed, the letters will complete a fact about South Dakota.

53

TeNnessee

Nickname: The Volunteer State | Capital: Nashville

Tulip tree | Iris | Mockingbird

Help this country western band make it to the Grand Ole Opry on time in the maze on the next page.

ROAD CLOSED

STOP

GRAND OLE OPRY

TeXas

Pecan | Bluebonnet | Mockingbird

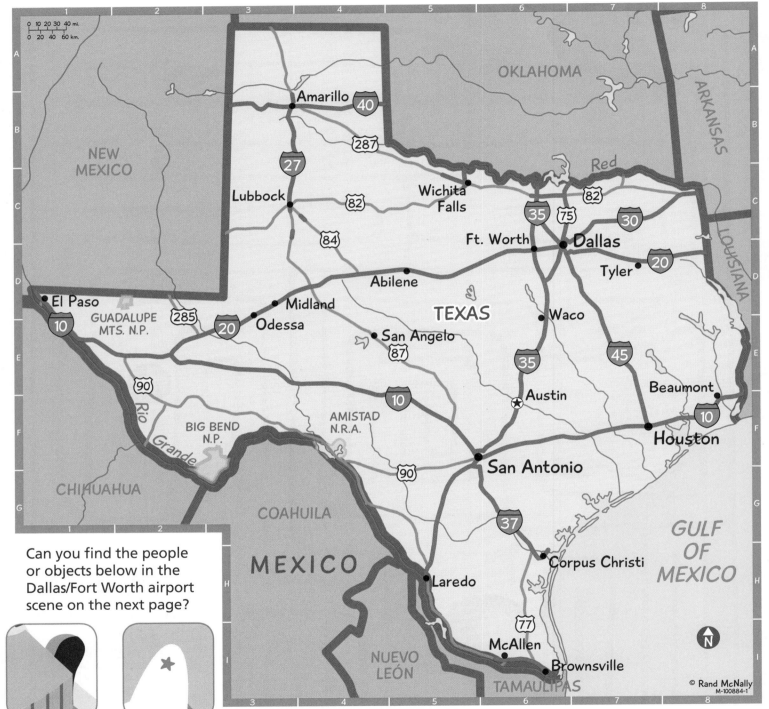

OKLAHOMA

NEW MEXICO

Amarillo 40

287

27

Lubbock

82

Wichita Falls

Red

82

35 75 30

ARKANSAS

Ft. Worth • Dallas

84

Tyler 20

Abilene

TEXAS

LOUISIANA

El Paso

GUADALUPE MTS. N.P.

285 Midland

10 20 Odessa

San Angelo

87

Waco

35

Beaumont

90

Rio Grande

BIG BEND N.P.

AMISTAD N.R.A.

10

45

10

Austin ★

Houston

90

San Antonio

CHIHUAHUA

COAHUILA

37

Corpus Christi

GULF OF MEXICO

MEXICO

Laredo

NUEVO LEÓN

77

McAllen

Brownsville

TAMAULIPAS

© Rand McNally
M-100884-1

N

Can you find the people or objects below in the Dallas/Fort Worth airport scene on the next page?

UTah

Nickname: The Beehive State | Capital: Salt Lake City

Blue spruce | Sego lily | American seagull

© Rand McNally
M-100893-1

Utah is home to many National Parks and Monuments. Circle the names, listed below the map, in the puzzle.

T	G	R	P	P	H	B	L	S	T	I	Y	T
T	L	I	N	E	S	A	R	C	H	E	S	C
A	E	B	A	O	R	E	Z	Q	R	O	M	H
Z	N	N	T	P	D	I	N	O	S	A	U	R
R	C	O	U	L	E	N	N	B	K	I	R	I
O	A	O	R	E	F	G	S	G	N	T	A	S
L	N	T	A	O	E	X	D	O	Z	B	D	Q
N	Y	F	L	F	G	G	I	L	L	I	B	K
G	O	G	B	E	C	W	N	D	A	W	O	E
L	N	K	R	A	P	S	H	E	C	V	Y	N
A	S	T	I	R	D	O	U	N	H	R	R	D
D	D	A	D	T	E	N	D	S	B	O	C	R
E	T	E	G	H	V	P	L	P	A	I	H	A
N	X	R	E	O	Y	T	S	I	M	I	S	I
S	O	R	S	K	B	R	A	K	N	S	O	V
C	A	P	I	T	O	L	R	E	E	F	G	S
M	G	I	L	K	B	I	I	J	R	I	O	O
A	Q	R	L	E	B	S	H	O	A	O	N	G
O	J	C	R	A	Y	A	D	C	L	N	A	H
C	A	N	Y	O	N	L	A	N	D	S	P	C
T	A	H	H	R	N	I	M	L	A	W	M	I
R	C	A	L	E	X	S	Y	T	L	P	I	N
S	K	A	E	R	B	R	A	D	E	C	T	C

ARCHES
CANYONLANDS
CAPITOL REEF
CEDAR BREAKS
DINOSAUR

GLEN CANYON
GOLDEN SPIKE
NATURAL BRIDGES
TIMPANOGOS
ZION

PARK PLACE

VermonT

Nickname: The Green Mountain State | Capital: Montpelier

Sugar maple | Red clover | Hermit thrush

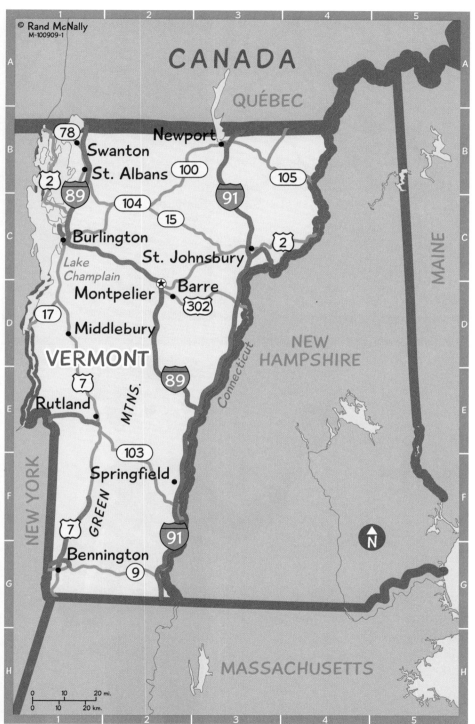

© Rand McNally
M-100909-1

CANADA
QUÉBEC
Newport
78
Swanton
St. Albans 100
104
15
Burlington
St. Johnsbury
Lake Champlain
Montpelier Barre
302
17
Middlebury
VERMONT
7
89
Rutland MTNS.
103
Springfield
GREEN
7
91
Bennington
9
MASSACHUSETTS
NEW YORK
MAINE
Connecticut
NEW HAMPSHIRE
91
105
2
89

0 10 20 mi.
0 10 20 km.

All of the facts about Vermont below are true...except for one. To find out which one is not true, solve the equation. The value of X will equal the number next to the false statement.

1. Native Americans taught Europeans how to tap maple trees for syrup.

2. Only Wyoming has fewer residents than Vermont.

3. Vermont was once its own country, with its own money!

4. Grandma Moses, a Vermont painter, worked until she was 101 years old.

5. Ice cream from Vermont is popular because cows there have a higher cream content in their milk.

X = The number of the false fact
$X = A - B + C$
$A = B + 4$
$B = C + 2$
$C = 1$

UNBELIEVABLE!

VirginiA

Nickname: Old Dominion | Capital: Richmond

Dogwood | Dogwood | Cardinal

© Rand McNally
M-100885-1

OHIO

WEST VIRGINIA

MARYLAND

SHENANDOAH N.P.

Washington

DEL.

81

95

Staunton

Charlottesville

KENTUCKY

64

29

James

64

Richmond

13

Chesapeake Bay

Lynchburg

Williamsburg

460

VIRGINIA

Roanoke

John H. Kerr Res.

85

Norfolk

460

ATLANTIC OCEAN

Abingdon

81

MT. ROGERS N.R.A.

Virginia Beach

TENNESSEE

NORTH CAROLINA

COLONiaL CLUes

This Virginia city was the center of politics and culture in colonial times. Use the clues to find out the name of this city.

1. It's about 50 miles southeast of Richmond.

2. It's about 35 miles northwest of Norfolk.

3. It's at coordinate C-7.

The city is _____

WAshington

Nickname: The Evergreen State | **Capital:** Olympia

 Western hemlock | Coast rhododendron | Willow goldfinch

Map features:
BRITISH COLUMBIA CANADA
Bellingham
NORTH CASCADES N.R.A.
ROSS LAKE N.R.A.
Oroville
395
20
Mt. Vernon
5
LAKE CHELAN N.R.A.
97
LAKE ROOSEVELT N.R.A.
Franklin D. Roosevelt Lake
20
Port Angeles
OLYMPIC N.P.
101
2
RANGE
155
Spokane
2
Seattle
OLYMPIC N.P.
101
Bremerton
16
90
Wenatchee
WASHINGTON
90
195
Tacoma
Olympia
410
MT. RAINIER N.P.
HANFORD REACH N.M.
17
127
Aberdeen
12
12
Yakima
12
PACIFIC OCEAN
4
5
MT. ST. HELENS NAT'L VOLCANIC MONUMENT
CASCADE
82
Kennewick
Walla Walla
Snake
Longview
97
Columbia
IDAHO
Vancouver
14
OREGON
N
© Rand McNally
M-100910-1

Picture Quiz

In the spaces provided, write the **last** letters of the objects shown in the boxes. When you're finished, the letters will spell out the name of an event that was started in 1909 by Sonora Louise Smart Dodd in Spokane, Washington.

___ ___ ___ ___ ___ ___ ___ ,

___ ___ ___

West Virginia

Sugar maple | Rhododendron | Cardinal

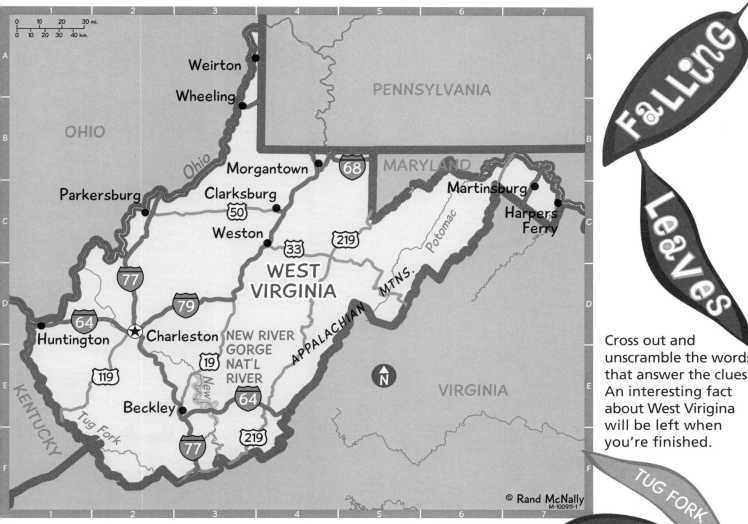

© Rand McNally
M-100911-1

Falling Leaves

Cross out and unscramble the words that answer the clues. An interesting fact about West Virigina will be left when you're finished.

TUG FORK
HARPERS FERRY
AMERICA'S
CHARLESTON
WEIRTON
NEW
RIVER
KENTUCKY
WESTON
THE
RIVER
IS
OHIO
POTOMAC
OLDEST

Clues

1. The town that is furthest north
2. The river that makes up most of the west border
3. The town that is "NOT SEW" scrambled
4. The river that begins with a "P"
5. The town that is the farthest east
6. The river that makes up part of the southwestern border
7. The state that borders West Virginia to the southwest
8. The state capital

63

WIsconsin

Sugar maple | Wood violet | Robin

© Rand McNally
M-100912-1

CLOWNING AROUND

In 1884, five brothers held their first circus with farm animals and jugglers in Wisconsin. Over time, it became the world-famous Ringling Brothers Circus. Find out what town held that first event and now has the Circus World Museum. Solve the puzzle below and read the one-letter answers from top to bottom.

1. A letter in BEAR, but not in TRAPEZE. _____
2. A letter in LAKE and MICHIGAN. _____
3. A letter in SPARTA and MERRILL. _____
4. A letter in SUGAR and MAPLE. _____
5. A letter in BRIE, but not in AMERICAN. _____
6. A letter in HOLSTEIN and COW. _____
7. A letter in TRACTOR, but not in CART. _____

WYoming

Cottonwood | Rhododendron | Western meadowlark

© Rand McNally
M-100871-1

MONTANA

212
BIGHORN CANYON N.R.A.
14
Sheridan
Devil's Tower National Monument
16 14 20
Cody
310
90
14 16
14
90
SOUTH DAKOTA
YELLOWSTONE NAT'L PARK
16
GRAND TETON N.P.
25
Gillette
26 287
Jackson
ROCKY MOUNTAINS
20
N. Platte
18 85
N
Riverton
20 26
WYOMING
Casper
NEBRASKA
89
189 191
220
IDAHO
28
287
Green River
30
Rawlins
30 287
85
UTAH
Evanston
80
Rock Springs
25
FLAMING GORGE N.R.A.
789
Laramie
Cheyenne
COLORADO

SEE YOU at the TOP!

Climb to the top! Start at the bottom left and see if you can make it to the top of Devil's Tower (A-7).

Canada

Capital: Ottawa

Take a Gander!

Hey! That Canadaian goose shouldn't be flying upside down! How many other mistakes can you find in the Canadian scene on the next page?

Mexico | Capital: Mexico City

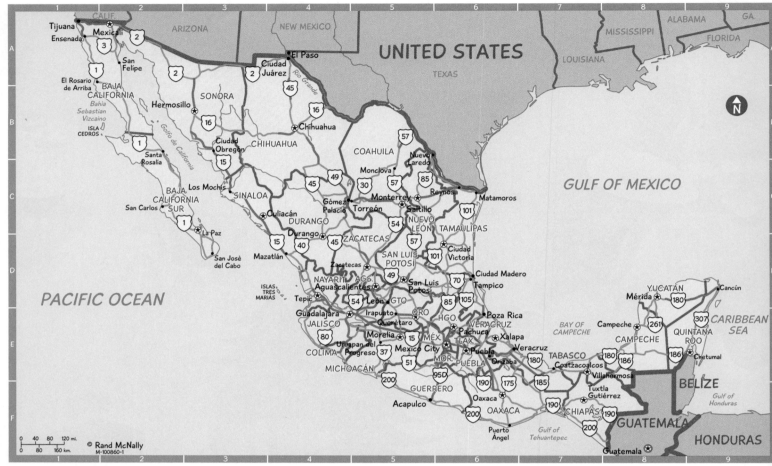

1. This body of water is to the east of Quintana Roo.

2. This city is in the northwest corner of the country.

3. This state on the south of the Bay of Campeche has the same name as a spicy sauce.

4. This food is a flat bread made from corn.

5. This river, or *rio*, forms much of the border between Mexico and the U.S.

6. This cliff-diving location is the southernmost point on highway 95D.

7. This city's name is a combination of Mexico and California.

8. This state in northern Mexico shares its name with a breed of dogs.

9. This body of water lies west of the Baja Peninsula.

10. This country lies east of Chiapas.

11. As you take highway 45 north, the last city you go through before leaving Mexico is _____.

12. This city is directly across the border to the north of question #11.

13. This country is south of Quintana Roo.

14. This "little beautiful" city is the capital city of the state of Sonora.

SOUTH OF the BORDER

Cross out the words in the puzzle that answer the questions on the opposite page. An interesting fact about Mexico will be left when you're finished. Read it from top to bottom.

MEXICANS

Tijuana
Belize
WERE
Acapulco
EL Paso
KNOWN
Ciudad Juárez
the
men
Mexicali
of
Hermosillo
Tabasco

Rio Grande

ONCE

CARIBBEAN SEA

GUATEMALA

CORN

TORTILLA

as

CHIHUAHUA

Pacific Ocean

License Plate Game

Keep an eye out for license plates from all over the United States. Cross off the state when you see its plate.

Alabama	Hawaii	Massachusetts	New Mexico	South Dakota
Alaska	Idaho	Michigan	New York	Tennessee
Arizona	Illinois	Minnesota	North Carolina	Texas
Arkansas	Indiana	Mississippi	North Dakota	Utah
California	Iowa	Missouri	Ohio	Vermont
Colorado	Kansas	Montana	Oklahoma	Virginia
Connecticut	Kentucky	Nebraska	Oregon	Washington
Delaware	Louisiana	Nevada	Pennsylvania	West Virginia
Florida	Maine	New Hampshire	Rhode Island	Wisconsin
Georgia	Maryland	New Jersey	South Carolina	Wyoming

are we there yet?

Contents

Don't miss your flight

Hurry and find your seat before the plane takes off!

Where are these travelers going?

Match the people waiting in the ticket line with their destination. Use the objects that the people are carrying and their clothing as clues.

Travel Time

1 ___
2 ___
3 ___
4 ___
5 ___

TICKETS

6 ___
7 ___
8 ___
9 ___

DESTINATIONS

A

B

C

D

E

F

G

H

I

Picture Park

Can you find the words hidden in the tree? Look across, up, down, backwards, and diagonally. All the words listed below are pictured on this page.

```
                    R I B   F
          A I C E   C R O E F R E A M   M
        W D T R T E   T S O I O   E N D
    I O A E T T   S T D A   L P C L
    G A N T R O T   B A L   L B   H
    B A S K E T B A L   L E   D N
    N F L O W E R S   R A O U R W S I K
    S I T H R S E M N E C R W   S I C
    S L A N U I T K E K T I A   I K C
    Q I T N P E L F L N O T   I A
    E U D N T E L I G O T N   I D
        N I E U T N S N E N   A D
        I E R U O E H P O N D
        E R T F E I N G
        S R   E F I N
                T F E L G
    P I E   N F N G
    I C   L C I   P
    C N   Y C I   O
    N I   C I B   L
    C     B     E X
```

dog
ice cream
bench
trees
blanket

runners
squirrel
bicycle
fishing pole
basketball

fountain
kite
pond
watermelon
flowers
slide

picnic
teeter-totter
radio
swing set
cooler
duck

75

You're bugging ME!

WHAT'S FOR LUNCH?

The bugs at your picnic have a message for you. Use the key to fill in the blanks.

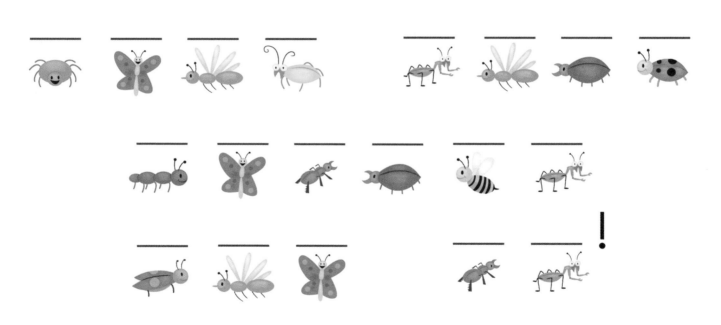

_ _ _ _ _ _ _ _

_ _ _ _ _ _ _ _ _ _ _

_ _ _   _ _ !

KEY

B C D E F M O P R S U

Souvenir......dot-to-dot...

Mom brought home a souvenir from her trip to New York City. Connect the dots in order from 1 to 71 to find out what it is.

·34

35· ·33

36· ·32

·31 ·30
30· ·37
·10 28 ·29   16   ·14
39   ·   ·   ·12
41· 27   18
·26
42· 25
43
                19· 17 13
                    15 ·
·24   ·10 ·9
                        ·8
44·   ·7
23· 22
45· 21 ·20

46· ·47
48·
·49

·50

·51

52·

·53

55· ·54   ·57
56·   58·   59   60

· I ♥ N Y ·

·5 ·3
·6
·4   ·2

71· ·1
·70

67· ·69
·66 68

·65

·64 ·63
·62
·61

77

Headline Adventure

Create your own wacky news story. Ask somebody for words
to fill in the blanks below. Then read the story aloud.

It was a _____ night and the _____ family was driving down the
ADJECTIVE (describing word)   NAME

highway on their way to _____. All of a sudden, they saw _____
PLACE   NUMBER

_____ along the side of the highway. They decided to _____
PLURAL NOUN   VERB

because it seemed like the right thing to do. _____ decided to call for a
NAME

little _____ and everyone else started _____. When the _____
NOUN   -ING WORD   NOUN

arrived, everything was under control. A passerby said, "It certainly was lucky that

this _____ family was driving by. Those kids knew exactly what to do in a
ADJECTIVE (describing word)

_____ like this. The kids admitted, "We were _____, and it was a
NOUN   ADJECTIVE (describing word)

great adventure, but now to have to get _____.
-ING WORD

Picture Postcard

On one side of the postcard, draw a picture from your trip. On the other side, write all about it.

To: _____

_____

_____

_____

Travel Journal

Today is _____

I am in _____

Best thing I did today: _____

Worst thing I did today: _____

_____

_____

Other Stuff

FUN-O-METER
TODAY IS...

FUN ↑ ↓ **NOT**

- WORDS FAIL!
- TOTALLY AWESOME
- COOL
- PRETTY FUN
- OK
- ZERO FUN
- BIG PAIN

MOOD CHECK

Today I feel...

- ☐ Cheerful
- ☐ Helpful
- ☐ Homesick
- ☐ Dopey
- ☐ Grumpy
- ☐ Sleepy
- ☐ Bashful
- ☐ Silly
- ☐ Bored
- ☐ Other

Weather -OR- NOT

Today's weather is...

Travel Tips

What are you favorite travel tips?
DRAW your own favorites or use ours!

Stake out your territory.

Show off your map reading skills.

Stay energized!

Summer Vacation Crossword Puzzle

ACROSS

1. Pool of rain in the street
4. Wheeled plank that "surfs" on sidewalk
9. Car without a roof
12. Short-sleeved cotton garment
14. Grassy area around a house
15. Napping spot that swings between two trees
17. Person who polices the beach
18. Inner _____ (fun float toy)
19. Crashing breakers at the ocean
21. Grass-watering sprayer
22. Rose or daisy

DOWN

1. Spiced cucumber sometimes eaten on hamburgers
2. Plunging into a pool off the board
3. Serving of corn on the cob
4. Water _____ ("ride" behind a boat)
5. Play home in the branches
6. Umpire's word in baseball
7. What to do when you're thirsty
8. Large, seedy summer fruit
10. Sport played with rackets and a net
11. To grill meat
13. Provides shade at the beach
16. Results of sitting in the sun
18. What to sit on at the beach
20. To jump rope

Tip-Top Travel Shop

Can you find 30 things in this scene that start with the letter T? Finding 15 is tricky, 20 is terrific, and 25 or more is tip-top.

Make me a map

The mapmaker went home early without finishing her job!
She drew 15 states, but forgot to label them.
Can you match the states with their names?

1. Florida _____

2. Michigan _____

3. Oklahoma _____

4. Ohio _____

5. Louisiana _____

6. California _____

7. Hawaii _____

8. Nevada _____

9. Virginia _____

10. Tennessee _____

11. Washington _____

12. New York _____

13. Utah _____

14. Massachusetts _____

15. Idaho _____

Auto Repair

This car needs a tune up. Can you unscramble the 14 parts listed below?

1. STRINGEE LEWEH _____
2. HODO _____
3. LACEORCRATE _____
4. KNURT _____
5. SWINDLEHID _____
6. BAKER _____
7. BRASHADDO _____

8. HEWEL _____
9. RIGHTSAFE _____
10. GENNIE _____
11. LADHEIGHT _____
12. BURPEM _____
13. ELFMURF _____
14. TYRETAB _____

Something's Fishy

Can you spot at least 10 differences between the top and bottom fish tanks?

Surf's UP!

Can you find 10 things wrong with this picture?

Travel Log

Write your own "been there, done that" lists under the headings below.

 I've been THERE

I've DONE that

 I'd like to go there

I NEVER want to go there

Wacky water park

Call the lifeguard! There's a whale in the swimming pool. That's not the only thing wrong at this water park. Look at the picture to find 11 other strange things.

TUBE SLIDE

PICNIC AREA

FUN TIMES WATER PARK

HOURS 9PM–6AM

On the Right Track

BOXCAR

BRAKEMAN

CABOOSE

CARGO

CATTLECAR

CHOO-CHOO

CONDUCTOR

CROSSING

ENGINEER

EXPRESS

LOCOMOTIVE

MONORAIL

PULLMAN

RAILROAD

ROUNDHOUSE

SIGNAL

TIES

TUNNEL

WHISTLE

The 19 words listed to the left are hidden in the train. Look across, back, up, down, and diagonally to find them.

Bloomers

How many flowers can you name using the word pictures below?

1. + =

2. + **E** =

3. + =

4. + =

5. + =

6. + **e** =

7. + =

8. + **n** + =

Winter Vacation

Crossword Puzzle

ACROSS

1. Hanukkah and Thanksgiving are two
4. Sled-pulling dog
8. Apple drink
10. Light coat
11. Pine trees, for instance
16. Head covering
18. Wax with a wick
19. Warm fabric for sheets or pajamas
20. Bed covering
21. Where to burn logs indoors
22. Twinkling light in the sky
23. Container that keeps drinks hot
24. The North _____ (Santa's home)

DOWN

1. Game played with a puck
2. Cozy inn
3. To glide on ice with blades
4. Sweet, warm drink
5. Frosty, for instance
6. Holiday word with log or -tide
7. Downhill or cross-country gliders
9. Floor covering
12. Rudolph, for instance
13. Travel on a snowmobile
14. Warm, knitted pullover
15. Sledded carrier pulled by horses
17. Hibernating

Highway Robbery

It was late in the afternoon as we sped along the dusty road in the family station wagon. We were on our way to Florida for our annual family vacation and my little sister Louise was really starting to get on my nerves. We were nearly to Chattanooga when the station wagon slowed down.

"What's going on?" my mother asked.

Through the windshield I could see some sort of roadblock. We slowly crept along until we reached several police officers standing by orange cones that blocked the road. An old blue convertible had been directed over to the side of the road and one of the officers was talking with the man who owned it.

My dad rolled down his window as another police officer approached our car.

"There's been a robbery at the local grocery store ten miles away," the officer explained. "We're checking cars, because we think the robber is trying to get out of town."

We all got out of the car. I sat on the bumper, listening to the conversation between the other policeman and the man in the blue convertible. I noticed that his backseat was filled with grocery bags.

"Officer, I tell you, these are my things I bought a day ago in Salt Lake City," the man said. "I've been driving for 12 hours straight. I haven't even heard of the grocery store you're talking about."

The policeman looked skeptical. He strolled to the front of the car, took out a notepad, and began writing down the license plate number on the convertible.

The man was not telling the truth.
Do you know what gave him away?

Happy Camper?

Help make this hungry camper a happy camper. Find the hidden fork, plate, cup, cooler, sandwich, apple, bottle of juice, and slice of cake.

Under the Big Top

Connect the dots in order from 1 to 109 to find out what the girl is riding.

Message in the Sand

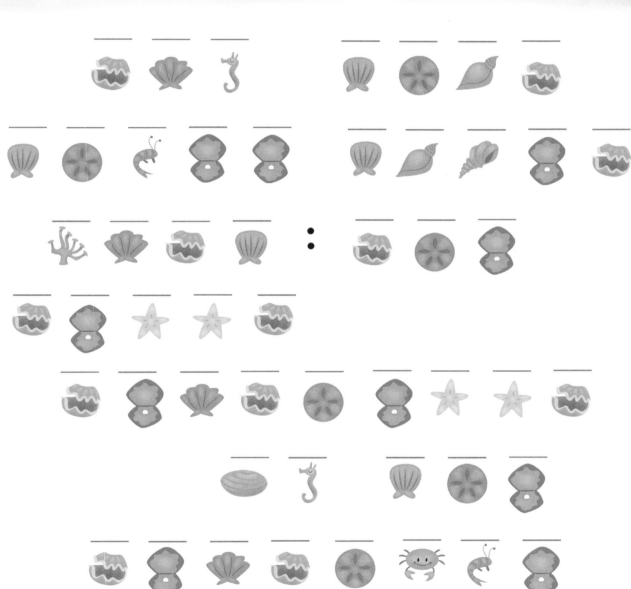

KEY

A B E F H I L M O R S T Y

Barnyard SCRAMBLE

How many of the 14 animal names can you unscramble?
All of the animals are pictured on this page.

1. GDO _____

2. ACT _____

3. OWC _____

4. ADOT _____

5. KUCD _____

6. TOGA _____

7. ORCW _____

8. OGSOE _____

9. EOMUS _____

10. SHOER _____

11. NOBRI _____

12. BRITAB _____

13. NARCOCO _____

14. RLIQEUSR _____

Backseat BINGO!

BINGO!

This game can be played with up to four people. Select a bingo card. Each time you see one of the items pictured on the card, draw an X on that square. The first person to cross out five squares across, down or diagonally wins.

Your friends have run off to their favorite rides at the amusement park. Use the nine squares below as hints to help you find your friends.

BUMPER CARS

TONS-O-FUN AMUSEMENT PARK

Travel Journal

Today is _____

I am in _____

Best thing I did today: _____

Worst thing I did today: _____

_____

_____

Other Stuff

FUN-O-METER
TODAY IS...

FUN

NOT

WORDS FAIL!

TOTALLY AWESOME

COOL

PRETTY FUN

OK

ZERO FUN

BIG PAIN

MOOD CHECK

Today I feel...

☐ Cheerful
☐ Helpful
☐ Homesick
☐ Dopey
☐ Grumpy
☐ Sleepy
☐ Bashful
☐ Silly
☐ Bored
☐ Other

Weather -OR- NOT

Today's weather is...

Fantasy Vacation

What's the best vacation you can imagine? Maybe it's sailing on the ocean, racing down the slopes, or even blasting off into space. Draw a picture of your very own fantasy vacation below.

Movie Set Match-up

There has been a mix-up on the movie set. See if you can help by matching the actors with their vehicles. Use the objects that the actors are carrying and their clothes as clues.

1. ____
2. ____
3. ____
4. ____
5. ____
6. ____
7. ____
8. ____
9. ____
10. ____

PROPS

A
B
C
D
E
F
G
H
I
J

MAIL

Start pedaling in Cape Cod, Massachusetts, and coast across the finish line in California. Watch out! There may be a few dead ends in your path.

The race is ON!

START

105

Plane Challenge

See if you can find a place in the puzzle for all of the words listed below. The numbers show you how many letters are in each word. Here's a hint: Start with the words that have 12, 14, or 16 letters in them. (Spaces between words don't count!)

3
hub
nap
sky

4
gate
ramp
soda
tags

5
aisle
coach
hotel
novel
pilot
seats
snack

6
laptop
pillow
on time
snooze
ticket

7
airport
blanket
co-pilot
deplane
parking
peanuts

8
airspeed
landings
navigate
schedule
takeoffs

9
concourse
passenger

10
first class
flight plan
turbulence

11
folding tray
landing gear

12
baggage check

13
inflight movie
ticket counter

14
carry-on luggage

15
baggage carousel
crossword puzzle
flight attendant

16
cruising altitude

Bicycle Mix-up

Looks like a bicycle mix-up. Can you find 10 other things wrong with this picture?

YIELD

BUY & BUY

You have exactly 205 tickets to spend on prizes. If you want to spend exactly all of your tickets and you don't want to buy more than one of anything, which items should you buy?

PRIZES

NECKLACES 80 TICKETS

POLISHED ROCKS 35 TICKETS

POSTCARDS 25 TICKETS

KEY RINGS 95 TICKETS

WINDUP TOY 50 TICKETS

GIANT PENCIL 70 TICKETS

CANDY 15 TICKETS

GLASSES 200 TICKETS

Which HOTEL?

It's getting late and the Tyred family needs to find their hotel. They know it's on Yawn Avenue, but which hotel is it? Mr. Tyred stayed here years ago and remembers the facts below. Use them to figure out where the family should check in before everyone falls asleep.

FACTS:

1. The hotel has a circular driveway.
2. The number on the hotel is even.
3. The hotel is between two hotels that have palm trees in front of them.
4. The name of the hotel (without the word "inn" or "hotel") spells another word when it is written backwards.

ZANY ZOO

Can you spot 10 differences between the top and bottom scenes?

While-you-wait BINGO!

BINGO!

This game can be played with up to four people. Select a bingo card. Each time you see one of the items pictured on the card, draw an X on that square. The first person to cross out five squares across, down or diagonally wins.

Best Vacation EVER!

Create your own crazy story. Ask somebody for words to fill in the blanks below. Then read the story aloud.

_____ says that the best vacation ever is a _____ trip to _____.
PERSON'S NAME   NOUN   PLACE

Once you're there, you just have to _____. And don't forget to _____. The most
                                                       VERB   VERB

exciting things to do are _____ and _____, but only if you're wearing _____.
                                      ACTIVITY   ACTIVITY   TYPE OF CLOTHING

There's _____ food to eat, too. Order the _____ and _____ special
              ACTIVITY (describing word)   NOUN   NOUN

for a real treat, and tell them _____ sent you. Before you head home, be sure to buy a
                                           PERSON'S NAME

_____ at the souvenir shop! It will always remind you of your _____ trip.
NOUN   ADJECTIVE (describing word)

Travel Journal

TODAY is _____

I am in _____

Best thing I did today: _____

Worst thing I did today: _____

_____

_____

Other Stuff

FUN-O-METER
TODAY IS...

FUN

NOT

WORDS FAIL!

TOTALLY AWESOME

COOL

PRETTY FUN

OK

ZERO FUN

BIG PAIN

MOOD CHECK

Today I feel...

☐ Cheerful
☐ Helpful
☐ Homesick
☐ Dopey
☐ Grumpy
☐ Sleepy
☐ Bashful
☐ Silly
☐ Bored
☐ Other

Weather -OR- NOT

Today's weather is...

Thumbs UP/Thumbs DOWN

List the best
of your trip
on this side.

List the worst
on this side.

Things to do

Souvenirs

People I've met

Food & Restaurants

Places to go

Soup's On

How many foods can you name using the pictures below?
You'll have to add and subtract letters or words to find the answers.

1. 🌱 + 🍃 + 🧈 + & + 🐙 - 🐟 =

2. 😄 BLAH BLAH BLAH + O =

3. M + 🧃 - B + A + 🛶 + 🦵 + & + 🥧 =

4. 🐶 ← - T + G + 🗑 - N + I =

5. 🦆 + ⛰ - 🧊 + 🧸 - F =

Stormy Seas

How many of these words can you unscramble? All 13 sea-going vessels are pictured above.

1. KAR _____
2. PISH _____
3. FRAT _____
4. OCEAN _____
5. CHATY _____
6. YAKKA _____
7. REBAG _____

8. BUGATTO _____
9. LOANDOG _____
10. ALSOBAIT _____
11. BRAINMUSE _____
12. WEIRDSNURF _____
13. CARRIFAT RICERRA _____

A few pointers

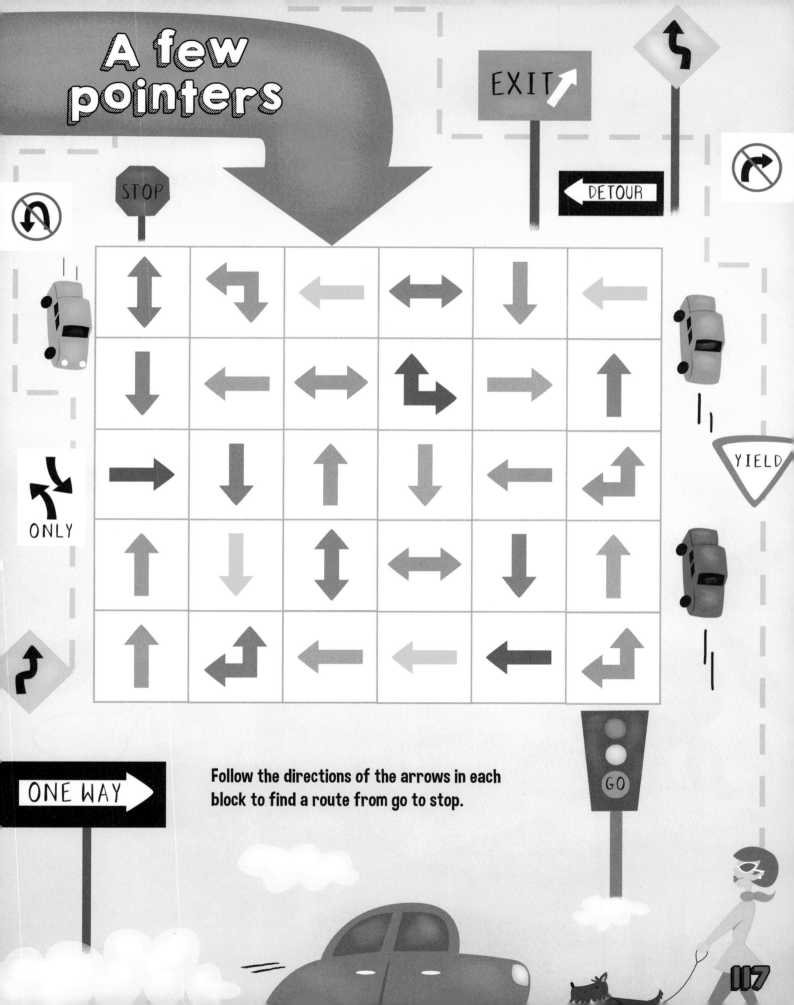

Follow the directions of the arrows in each block to find a route from go to stop.

The conveyor belt is going too fast, and the luggage has spilled all over the floor. Can you help the musician find her headphones, harmonica, sheet music, compact discs, and horn?

Mini-mystery

SEA BREEZE HOTEL

Pooltime Puzzler

It was a sunny morning and I was lounging by the pool at our hotel. We had arrived in Florida yesterday and were taking it easy. The drive to Florida had taken longer than usual, because we got stuck in a roadblock on the way down.

My dad was in the pool, splashing around with my little sister Louise. My mom was stretched out on the lounge chair next to me, reading a book.

"Plunk." A tall woman with flaming red hair and long, sparkly earrings sat down in the chair on the other side of me.

"How ya doin,' darlin'?" she asked in a slow drawl. "I'm visiting my son, who moved here last year from our home state of North Carolina."

"I'm here with my mom and dad...and my little sister," I said.

"Oh, a sister," the lady said, "that's nice. Girls run in my family, too. I don't have a brother, but I do have a sister, who has no children." She continued, "My sister's father had a wife whose mother had a great grandaughter with a twin sister. But, the twins had no brothers."

Across the pool, someone yelled to the lady. "Peaches, I'm ready to go."

The lady smiled, got up, and said, "It's a nickname my son has for me. You know, like the nickname of my home state. Now you have a nice visit down here and take care of your little sister."

She walked away and I turned to my mom: "The lady with the red hair has a lot of imagination. But she doesn't have a son and she isn't from North Carolina."

Do you know how I figured this out?

dot-to-dot... Down Under

Connect the dots in order from 1 to 87 to find out what's pulling the carriage.

Skiing Double

A.

B.

C.

D.

E.

F.

G.

H.

Can you spot the two skiers that are exactly alike?

Up, up & away!

flying
gate
hop
hub

clouds
cockpit
crew
departure
estimated time of arrival
flight

jet
landing
navigate
passenger

seat
sky
snack
tags
takeoff
ticket

peanuts
pillow
pilot
radar
row
schedule

aisle
airline
airplane
airport
arrival
bags
cabin

time
turbulence
weather
wings

All of the words listed in the clouds are hidden in the airplane. Look across, down, up, backwards, and diagonally to find them.

Where's my mummy?

You're lost in the museum. Can you find your way from the dinosaurs to the gift shop?

ENTER HERE →

GIFT SHOP

Hide and Seek

These kids are playing hide and seek in their hotel room. Can you spy these items hidden in the room with them: a magnifying glass, umbrella, snake, hot dog, skateboard, baseball cap, book, and donut?

Flag Code

Use the International Flag Code to solve the riddle below.

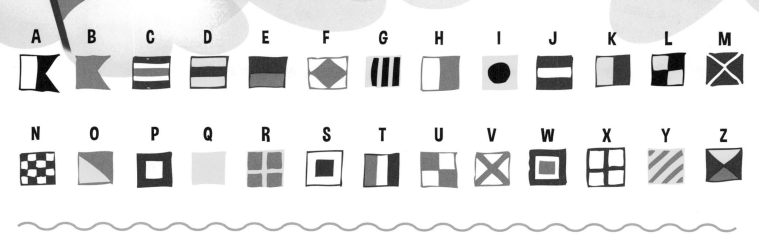

A B C D E F G H I J K L M

N O P Q R S T U V W X Y Z

125

I SPY

If you are "it," choose an object, like a red button, and say, "I spy with my little eye something red." The other players then take turns trying to guess what the object is. The person who guesses the answer gets to be "it." HINT: Don't give the answer away by staring at the object.

MAKE ME LAUGH

This game is serious fun. No kidding! One person becomes the "jester" and the rest are "stonefaces." Stonefaces must never laugh or smile—if they do, their faces break. Of course the jester thinks this is funny and likes nothing more than to make stonefaces crack up. That's the game! The jester has to crack up the stonefaces. The jester can make faces, funny noises, tell jokes, but cannot tickle or touch the stonefaces to make them laugh. The last stoneface to laugh gets to be the next jester.

ROCHAMBEAU

This game, sometimes called "Rock, Paper, Scissors," works best with two or three players. These are the rules—paper (flat hand) covers rock, rock (fist) breaks scissors, and scissors (move first two fingers like scissors) cut paper. All players put their fists out together to the beat of Rochambeau (Ro—Sham—Bo). On "Bo," each player forms either rock, paper, or scissors. Then everybody has to follow the rules.

NAME THAT TUNE

Players take turns thinking of songs and humming them for one another, a few notes at a time, while the others try to be the first to "name that tune." Once you have a tune in mind, hum just the first three notes. If nobody recognizes it, hum the first four notes. Keep adding notes, one at a time, until someone guesses the name of the song. The first person to guess becomes the next "hummer."
(Good whistlers can whistle their tunes.)

CITY TRAIN

If you know the names of a lot of cities, take a ride on the City Train. The rules are simple—players take turns saying the names of cities. The only catch is that each city name must begin with the letter that ended the last one. For example, Houston might be followed by New York, which might be followed by Kansas City, and so on. Any player who can't come up with a city has to get off the train. The last one riding the City Train is the winner. All aboard!

Travel Games

A—MY NAME IS...

Here's a "fill in the blank" game that works its way through the alphabet. It's best when the pressure of keeping the rhythm going makes players work especially hard. Here's how a boy might start things off beginning with the letter A: A—my name is Abner, my sister's name is Anne, we come from Alaska and we sell Axes." A girl might follow, "B—my name is Bertha, my brother's name is Bert, we come from Boston and we sell beans." You get the idea—you're out when you can't complete the sentence or when you break the tempo.

PLATE-O-GRAMS

This game has no winner or losers—just some funny messages. To start, somebody has to spot a license plate and read the letters on the plate to everyone. For example, the letters might be "B—R—G." Next, everyone thinks of a three-word message beginning with those letters. In this case, people might come up with "<u>B</u>ig <u>R</u>ound <u>G</u>lobs" or "<u>B</u>eware <u>R</u>abid <u>G</u>erbils." (You might want to allow "little" words so the plate-o-grams make more sense, for example, "My <u>B</u>rother is <u>R</u>eally <u>G</u>ross.")

ALPHABET DERBY

This is a race to the end of the alphabet. To play, you must find all the letters of the alphabet—in order. Letters may be found on road signs, billboards, bumper stickers, license plates, etc. You don't have to announce each letter you find, but if asked, you must tell what letter you are on. If challenged, you should be able to say where you saw your letters. The first one to Z wins. (To make things go more quickly, you may want to agree that Q is the only letter that can be found out of order.)

BUZZ

If you've got a head for numbers, buzz is for you. First, players pick a number from 2 through 9. That number becomes buzz. Once buzz is named, players take turns counting, starting with 1. If buzz is 3, whenever you get to a number that contains a 3 or is a multiple of 3, you must say buzz. Players who mess up are out and counting starts over again from 1. The last player remaining wins. For a challenge, play bizz-buzz, picking two numbers instead of just one. One number is bizz, and the other is buzz.

CATEGORIES

This game is good for many ages, since it can be made as easy or as difficult as you want. It all has to do with categories. One person thinks of a category—any category. It could be colors, capital cities, sports teams, or anything you can think of. Then players take turns naming items in the category. The game ends when someone repeats something already mentioned, or when players can't think of any other items in the category.

20 QUESTIONS

This old standby is simple, but fun. One player thinks of something (anything you can see, smell, hear, or touch) and tells the others if it is an animal, vegetable, or mineral. The others take turns asking "yes—or—no" questions to try to figure out what it is. At any time a player may use a turn to guess what it is. It's best to ask a lot of questions before you start guessing, but remember, you only have twenty questions. Whoever guesses right wins. You can play this game using other categories, too, like famous people, places, etc. Be creative!

The Twelve Days of Our Trip
(to the tune of "The Twelve Days of Christmas")

On the first day of our trip this is what I saw—
the baby throw up in the car.

On the second day of our trip this is what I saw—
two pick-up trucks and the baby throw up in the car.

Third day: three dead skunks
Fourth day: four minivans
Fifth day: five backseat fights
Sixth day: six broken headlights
Seventh day: seven miles of road work
Eighth day: eight cars a-speeding
Ninth day: nine railroad crossings
Tenth day: ten roadside rest stops
Eleventh day: eleven cop cars hiding
Twelfth day: twelve bumper stickers

99 Miles to Go on Our Trip
(to the tune of "99 Bottles")

99 miles to go on our trip.
99 miles to go.
Step on the gas. I think we can pass.
98 miles to go on our trip…

(Keep repeating until you get to "0 miles to go" or until someone kicks you out of the car, whichever comes first.)

Songs to drive

Backseat Border Blues
(to the tune of "This Land is Your Land")

This side is my side; that side is your side.
Let's get along now; this is a long ride.
You see this line here—please don't cross over.
One side for you and one for me.

I had my eyes closed—faked I was sleeping.
So you got greedy and started creeping.
Try that again, Bub, and you'll be weeping.
One side for you and one for me.

Just like I warned you—now you are crying.
And Dad is angry—now you are lying.
You had it coming, there's no denying.
One side for you and one for me.

grown-ups CRAZY!

Are We Lost?
(to the tune of "Are you Sleeping?")

Are we lost? Are we lost?
Yes we are. Yes we are.
Someone get a map out. Someone get a map out.
Find the way. Find the way.

(Save this one for when you really get lost. Sing it as a round—as you drive around and around—and you're sure to drive the grown-ups crazy.)

DETOUR

Don't Get Out of the Fast Lane
(to the tune of "Take Me Out to the Ball Game")

Don't get out of the fast lane.
Don't let up on the gas.
I can't believe all the cars we've passed—
Wherever we're going, we're going there fast.
And it's zoom, zoom, zoom down the freeway.
But don't break the speed limit please.
Or the friend-ly Highway Patrol
Will request your keys!

Battle Hymn of the Brat
(to the tune of "Battle Hymn of the Republic")

Our minivan is loaded to the roof with games and toys.
We've all had snacks and found a station everyone enjoys.
The kids are all behaving well; we've hardly made a noise.
But something's not quite right.

(Chorus)
I'M NOT HAVING ANY FUN YET.
I'M NOT HAVING ANY FUN YET.
I'M NOT HAVING ANY FUN YET.
THIS TRIP IS DRAGGING ON.

We've hit every tourist trap from Maine to Monterey.
Miami to Mount Rushmore, Plymouth Rock to Frisco Bay.
We wait in never-ending lines forever and a day.
It's time to take a rest.

(Chorus)

Now you might think that I'm spoiled, that my attitude is bad.
You wouldn't be the first if my complaining makes you mad
In fact you'd be the third, behind my Mother and my Dad.
But I still feel like this:

(Chorus)

When-You-Get-There

Paper Airplane Games

Find some paper and follow the paper airplane instructions. Then you can play games with your paper planes. 1) Go for distance. Whose plane can fly the farthest? 2) Fly for accuracy. Who can land closest to a chosen target? 3) Stay aloft. Whose plane can stay in the air the longest?

FOLD, THEN UNFOLD ON ①

FOLD DOWN CORNERS
FOLD DOWN ON LINE ②

FOLD DOWN CORNERS AGAIN

FOLD LITTLE FLAP UP

FOLD THIS SIDE BACK TO MEET OTHER SIDE

FOLD WINGS DOWN ON BOTH SIDES

Bright Ideas

If you have a flashlight, you will never be bored again, at least not until you wear the batter out. Set up a flashlight in a dark room and make hand shadow figures on the wall. Tell a scary story while projecting a spider or a ghost onto the ceiling. Cut out shadow puppets and put on a show. With more than one flashlight you can play flashlight tag after dark—instead of tagging people, you hit them with your beam of light. A flashlight can also add a scary touch to face-making. Turn out the lights and see how scary you can look!

Hide the Doohickey

Any small object will do in this game. It's fun for kids of all ages. One player hides the object while the others wait in another room. Players are then called back to find the object. Younger players might need to be told if they are "warm" or "cold." The first player to find the object gets to hide it next.

Learn to Girn

Face facts, faces are funny. Take your face to a mirror and see just how funny it can get. Serious face-makers call it "girning." It's even funnier if you have someone else to girn with. Work on blinks, winks, sneers, grimaces, grins, eyebrow raises, sidelong glances, etc. How many emotions can you show? How many faces can you make?

GAMES

Wastebasket H-O-R-S-E
A wastebasket makes a good indoor basketball hoop, and horse is a good indoor game. In horse, players take turns shooting for the hoop from various places on the court. Use rolled-up socks, crumpled-up paper or an appropriate indoor ball. If a player makes a shot the next player must make it too. One miss, and you get an H, two misses, an H-O; and so on. Miss five times and you are out with H-O-R-S-E.

Sock Soccer
This game is just like it sounds. Roll up some socks, set up some goals, agree on a rule or two, and start kicking. (WARNING: According to the American Sock Soccer Association, using lamps and plants for goalposts can get you in an awful lot of trouble!)

Slo-mo Volleyball
If you have any balloons left over from the water balloon toss, fill one with air for this slow motion indoor version of volleyball. Play on your knees using a bed, couch, or some chairs for a net. You give up a point when you hit the balloon out, let it touch the ground, or fail to get it over in the agreed upon number of hits. Spike it, dude, but don't let it pop!

Water Balloon Toss
In this damp contest, players pair up and form two lines facing each other. Each pair gets a balloon. One at a time, one person in each pair tosses the balloon to the other. After each successful toss, the tosser backs up a full step. The pair completing the longest toss wins and gets to stay dry! Most grown-ups will insist that you play this game outside.

Whirly-Bird
Make a simple paper helicopter using the instructions. Decorate your whirly-bird with markers or crayons before you cut it out. Drop your whirly-bird from a high place. When the wind is right, your whirly-bird will stay in the air for a long time. Watch it land, and then be sure to get it and fly it again.

CUT AT 1, 2, 3

FOLD
A BACK
B FORWARD
C AS SHOWN

FOLD UP

Where oh where?

The pictures below appear somewhere in this book—but where? Find each picture and write the title of the page it appears on in the blanks. Then write the circled letters in order at the bottom of the page to decode the hidden message.

132

Contents

With *Coast-to-Coast Games* you can discover exciting new adventures, coast to coast and border to border within the United States. Check out the great scenery and terrific things to see and do, and meet some interesting people. It's time to explore these fun kid-friendly places along the way.

This book will tell you about many of these places. Read a little, play the games, and pretend that you are there. The United States map at the beginning of this book will show you where these places are located. Look into the ones that are near your home, or plan to visit the places that seem fun to you. Be sure to watch for the little red bird throughout this book for special surprises.

The travel games will make the time fly as you ride along in the car or fly in an airplane. Play the games alone or with other people. The games range from easy to hard, but all of them are fun. The only supplies you need are a pencil, crayons, and coins or other markers.

So grab your book and supplies, buckle up, and you're off on a great adventure "coast to coast."

CANADA

MINNESOTA
Duluth

Lake Superior

WISCONSIN

Minneapolis/
St. Paul

Wisconsin Dells
Milwaukee

IOWA

Chicago

ILLINOIS

Lake Michigan

Lake Huron

MICHIGAN

Dearborn

Detroit

Cleveland

OHIO

Indianapolis

INDIANA

Cincinnati

Louisville

Bluegrass
Country

KENTUCKY

Mammoth
Cave N.P.

as City

MISSOURI

St. Louis

Ozarks

Little
Rock

ARKANSAS

MISSISSIPPI

Natchez

LOUISIANA

ton

New
Orleans

GULF OF MEXICO

Lake Erie

Lake Ontario

Niagara
Falls

PENNSYLVANIA

Pittsburgh

Lancaster

Valley
Forge

NEW JERSEY

Philadelphia

Baltimore

DELAWARE

MARYLAND

Washington
D.C.

WEST
VIRGINIA

Williamsburg

Jamestown

Richmond

VIRGINIA

NORTH
CAROLINA

Charlotte

Cape Hatteras

Great Smoky
Mtns. N.P.

Nashville

TENNESSEE

Huntsville

Atlanta

SOUTH
CAROLINA

Charleston

GEORGIA

ALABAMA

St. Augustine

Cape Kennedy/
Titusville

Central Florida/
Orlando

Tampa/
St. Petersburg

FLORIDA

Miami

Everglades N.P.

BAHAMAS

MAINE

Arcadia N.P.

VT.

NEW
YORK

N.H.

Portland

Boston
Plymouth

MASS.

Cape Cod

CONN.

R.I.

Mystic

New York

ATLANTIC
OCEAN

Guide to Adventure

Symbols

✳ Terrific Place

• City

Regions

  Middle Atlantic

  Midwest

  Northeast

  Pacific Coast &
  Northern Rocky Mountains

  South

  Southwest

Abbreviations

N.P. National Park

N.M. National Monument

N

Hawaii's Volcanoes

Look into a volcano at Hawaii Volcanoes National Park and imagine how the world looked long ago. Stand at the rim—but be careful! Down below a fiery pit glows with power...black lava rock twists its way through a strange, bare land...and puffs of evil-smelling steam escape from cracks in the ground.

Did You Know?

The big island of Hawaii is the youngest of the present Hawaiian islands. But, to the southeast of Hawaii, under the water, is a new volcanic island forming which should reach the surface in about 10,000 years.

Can you identify the parts of a volcano?

Cinder cone___-_____   Lava_____

Crater_____   Magma_____

Eruption_____   Vent_____

Gas and ash_____   Volcanic bombs_____

Denali National Park

Where's the highest mountain in North America? Right here! Mt. McKinley is so tall (20,320 feet) that its peak is nearly always covered by clouds. Walking on the tundra feels strange—it's bouncy. Don't forget to bring binoculars to spy on the grizzly bears and other wild animals.

Alaska

Midnight Sun!

Find and circle these things you can see in Denali.

Arctic Warbler	Marmot
Bear	Moose
Beaver	Mountain Goat
Caribou	Mount McKinley
Cliff	Otter
Cub	Pika
Dall Sheep	Ptarmigan
Fox	Raven
Glacier	River
Golden Eagle	Rock
Golden Plover	Snow Bunting
Grebe	Snowshoe Hare
Grizzly Bear	Spruce
Hill	Squirrel
Ice	Tern
Log	Valley
Long-Tailed Jaeger	Wheatear
Loon	Wolf
Lynx	Wolverine

L	O	O	N	G	G	N	I	T	N	U	B	W	O	N	S
L	O	N	N	A	G	I	M	R	A	T	P	O	W	P	R
E	O	N	R	A	S	Q	U	I	R	R	E	L	H	E	T
Y	N	G	G	E	O	R	E	V	I	R	L	V	E	E	A
E	R	R	O	T	T	E	R	A	T	I	T	E	A	H	R
L	E	E	Y	L	A	H	K	E	H	A	R	R	T	S	C
N	L	B	E	N	D	I	E	S	O	O	M	I	E	L	T
I	G	E	L	A	P	E	L	G	D	R	N	N	A	L	I
K	A	L	L	E	V	E	N	E	M	F	E	E	R	A	C
C	E	R	A	E	C	I	U	P	D	A	F	V	V	D	W
M	N	A	V	C	A	U	C	O	L	J	R	I	A	A	A
T	E	E	F	T	I	U	R	Y	B	O	A	M	L	E	R
N	D	B	N	L	B	E	N	P	N	I	V	E	O	C	B
U	L	U	T	F	O	X	R	U	S	R	R	E	G	T	L
O	O	E	S	N	O	W	S	H	O	E	H	A	R	E	E
M	G	R	I	Z	Z	L	Y	B	E	A	R	O	C	K	R

Ever eat in a moving restaurant? There are two of them at the top of the 605-foot Space Needle. Look down on the city, then get down and explore the tide pools, astro-space displays, and more at the Pacific Science Center. Ride the monorail downtown, eat your way through Pike Place Market, then take a boat ride around Puget Sound.

Seattle

Washington

Waterfront Wonders!
See the Seattle waterfront's great scenery, sights, and shopping. Four miles long, start at either end.

7 **Waterfront Park–**
Fishing, scenery, picnicking

8 **The Seattle Aquarium–**
Dome puts you underwater for a fish-eye view

9 **Pike Street Hillclimb–**
157 steps up to fascinating...

10 **Pike Place Market–**
Longest continuously operating farmers' market in the U.S.

1 **King Street Station–**
Historic train station

2 **Klondike Gold Rush National Historical Park–**
See things needed by miners heading to the Klondike gold fields in Alaska and Canada in 1897–98

3 **Pioneer Square–**
Heart of Old Seattle; see the totem pole

4 **Washington State Ferry Terminal–**
Ferries leave for many places including Canada

5 **Seattle Harbor Tours–**
Take a tour of the harbor, Pier 55

6 **Pier 56–**
Tours to Tillicum Indian Village at Blake Island State Park

Rogue River

Black bears, river otters, and bald eagles hunt and play along the Rogue River. Look for them as you travel this wild, watery, "road." You might choose to bounce through the tumbling water in a rubber raft. Or, would you rather roar and splash your way upstream in a jet boat?

Oregon

Backseat Bingo!

As you ride along, when you see one of these things, mark the picture square on your card. If you see a horse, mark the square with a horse on it. To play alone, pretend you are playing with a friend, and see who wins. The first filled row of squares diagonally, up and down, or across is the winner.

141

Yellowstone/Grand Teton National Parks

Wyoming

The oldest national park has...Old Faithful! This famous geyser shoots water more than a hundred feet into the air. Mudpots pop and plop their oozy contents out like little volcanoes. And hot springs spread out like spilled paint—bright blue, green, orange, and yellow. Look out for the bears!

Hot Stuff!

Do you know what to look for in Yellowstone Park? Crack the code to see!

YOZXP YVZI_____

TVBHVIH_____

YRHLM_____

NZNNLGS SLG HKIRMTH_____

TIRAAOB YVZI_____

NLLHV_____

VOP (DZKRGR)_____

ZMGVOLKV_____

YRTSLIM HSVVK_____

BVOOLDHGLMV UZOOH_____

YZOW VZTOV_____

LOW UZRGSUFO_____

KZRMG KLGH_____

YVZEVI_____

A	B	C	D	E	F	G	H	I	J	K	L	M
Z	Y	X	W	V	U	T	S	R	Q	P	O	N

N	O	P	Q	R	S	T	U	V	W	X	Y	Z
M	L	K	J	I	H	G	F	E	D	C	B	A

Grand Teton National Park

Time for some exercise! Hiking and mountain climbing are the best ways to enjoy the wild scenery of this park. Keep an eye out for moose—they're everywhere. When you're tired or just for fun, relax with a float trip on the Snake River. Or, take a boat ride around Jackson Lake. In Jackson Hole, the winter skiing is great and it is fun to watch the huge local elk herd check in for a free lunch.

Riddle Time!

What has banks, but no money?_____

What has legs, but can't walk?_____

What has eyes, but can't see?_____

What has a bed, but never sleeps?_____

What has arms, but can't hug?_____

What has hands, but can't clap?_____

What has a face, but no head?_____

What has a mouth, but never smiles?_____

What has heels, but no feet?_____

What has a head and foot, but no body?_____

What has a neck, but no head?_____

What has an elbow, but no arm?_____

What has knees, but no legs?_____

What has ears, but can't hear?_____

What has fingers, but can't type?_____

Glacier National Park

Want to make snowballs in summer? In this park, summer isn't just for flowers. Snow lays scattered over the ground all year. Huge rivers of ice called glaciers creep over the land, slower than a snail. Hike the trails and try to spot bighorn sheep or mountain goats before they spot you.

Montana

Stash your trash!

The national parks are our wonderful heritage. Lets keep them clean and beautiful. Draw a line from each item to its environmental lifetime.

1 month

3 months

200-500 years

Over 500 years

As much as 1,000,000 years, (maybe never!)

Lake Tahoe

California

Nevada

Boat or "fly," sail or slide. This mountain lake is fun to visit year round. In the summer, hit the beaches for swimming, boating, or parasailing. In the winter, head for the mountain slopes surrounding Lake Tahoe. The snow is deep and the skiing is great!

What Can You Do at Lake Tahoe?

Fill in the fun activities from the clues. When you finish, the letters in the boxes will tell you where you are.

— — ▢ —

— — — — — ▢ — —

— — ▢ —

— — — ▢

— — — — — ▢ —

— — ▢ — —

— — ▢ —

— — ▢ —

— — — — ▢ — — —

Played with a club and small ball

Glide on an ice rink

Downhill or cross-country

Gallop on a horse

You need a racket, ball, and net

Go in a boat without a motor

A walk in the outdoors

Rides on the water

Ride on the water behind a boat

Did You Know?
Lake Tahoe, a magnificent emerald-colored mountain lake located in two states, is 6,229 feet high, up to 1,640 feet deep, and 193 square miles in area.

Roller coaster up and down the city hills on the cable cars. Wiggle your way along Lombard Street, the most twisty street in the world. Find chicken feet for sale in Chinatown and crabs at Fisherman's Wharf. Explore gardens and an aquarium in Golden Gate Park, or the old prison on Alcatraz Island.

San Francisco

Did You Know?

The Golden Gate Bridge:
- is not gold but red
- has towers 746 feet high
- has a 4,200-foot main span
- is 1.7 miles long (8,981 feet)
- has main support cables 3 feet in diameter
- needs 60,000 gallons of paint to paint it

California

Hit the Road!

If you are traveling on I-80 from New York City to San Francisco, through how many states will you pass?_____

What are they? Use the map on pages 4 and 5.

_____ _____
_____ _____
_____ _____
_____ _____
_____ _____

Yosemite National Park

California

Look up and up and up! Everything here is taller than tall. The rock cliffs and peaks push at the sky. Waterfalls look as if they are falling from the clouds. Even the trees are huge—especially the Grizzly Giant! The Pioneer History Center and the Indian Museum bring back the olden days.

All Aboard!

Yosemite is full of wonderful things to see and do. Fill in the puzzle to learn what some of them are.

Nut	Canyon
Fern	Meadow
Hike	Merced
Lake	Camping
Pass	Sequoia
Peak	Sierras
Roam	Ahwahnee
Rock	Half Dome
Tree	Mariposa
Vale	Mountain
View	Tuolumne
Eagle	Edyth Lake
Trail	El Capitan
	Yosemite Falls

HOLLYWOOD

Los Angeles

California

You can quiver through an earthquake at Universal Studios and meet Mickey Mouse at Disneyland. See tar pits that trapped prehistoric beasts. Shop at a Mexican street market in Old Los Angeles. Visit Griffith Park to roam the zoo, ride a merry-go-round, or see stars in the planetarium.

Cars, cars, and more cars!

Fill in these words that begin with C A R.

C A R __ __ __ __   A chewy treat

C A R __ __ __ __   Seeds found in rye bread

C A R __ __ __ __ __ __ __   Part of a car's engine

C A R __ __   There are 52 in a deck

C A R __ __ __ __ __   A bright red bird

C A R __ __ __ __   Watch out!

C A R __ __ __ __ __   Lots of rides and fun

C A R __ __ __ __ __   Merry-go-round

C A R __ __ __ __ __ __   He works with a hammer and nails

C A R __ __ __   A large rug

C A R __ __ __ __ __   Babies ride in style

C A R __ __ __   A rabbit's favorite food

C A R __ __ __   A cardboard box

Round and Round She Goes!

Hop aboard the ferris wheel to discover things to see in Los Angeles. The letters you need to crack the code are red.

TJOYRCDZYT _____

FYWMM'O XRQQC _____

   PZQB _____

LWDDCGWWT _____

PZQBRQ'O BZQFRM _____

ORZ GWQDT _____

QZYVLW DZ XQRZ MZQ _____

   UJMO _____

LWDDCGWWT XWGD _____

OJE PDZNO BZNJV _____

   BWKYMZJY _____

KYJIRQOZD OMKTJWO

   LWDDCGWWT _____

SKRRY BZQC _____

XRIRQDC LJDDO _____

QWOR XWGD _____

NRYR ZKMQC GROMRQY

   LRQJMZNR BKORKB _____

YXV OMKTJWO _____

NQJPPJML UZQF

   WXORQIZMWQC _____

MLR VWDJORKB _____

149

Sequoia/Kings Canyon National Parks

California

Tree Ring Circus!

Some of California's trees are very big and very old. Count the rings of each of these trees to tell how old. Which two tree sections are from the same tree? Don't forget to count the middle.

You'll feel as small as an ant when you walk through the giant forest of sequoia trees (named for the Indian chief Sequoyah). The General Sherman tree is the largest living tree in the world—taller than a 25-story building. You can also see a real cabin built in a hollow log and tour Crystal Cave.

San Diego

California

Have fun that's wet and wild! Look a shark in the eye and feed a dolphin at Sea World, or hit the beaches. Explore a jungle at the zoo and watch wild animals on the loose at the Wild Animal Park. If you like planes, trains, dinosaurs, or science, check out the fun at the museums in Balboa Park.

Do the Zoo, San Diego That Is!

Who has the longest neck?

Who has the longest nose?

Who can run the fastest?

Who is the King of the Beasts?

Who is the horse in striped pajamas?

Who can hang by his tail?

Who comes with her own pocket?

Who is called a river horse?

Salt Lake City

Utah

Bob like a beach ball in the Great Salt Lake or catch the waves at Raging Water Theme Park. Head for the 49th Street Galleria for games, rides, and even more fun. Time travel back to pioneer days with a visit to Old Deseret Village or count the organ pipes at the Mormon Tabernacle. Look for the Seagull Monument. This bird is very special to the city.

Capital Place!

How much do you know about our state capitals? Try this quiz and see!

1. What two state names are found in the names of their state capitals?

2. In which state capital is the U.S. Naval Academy located?

3. What capital name means "red stick" in French?

4. What state capital is named for our 16th president?

5. Which state capital is known as "Music City?"

6. What four states and their capitals begin with the same letter?

7. Which state capital can only be reached by plane or boat?

8. Name six state capitals that begin with "s."

9. Which state capital has the longest history?

10. Which state capital means "stone" in French?

Did You Know?
The Great Salt Lake is the second saltiest body of water in the world, after the Dead Sea, between 6 and 27 percent salt. Makes floating very easy!

152

Dinosaur National Monument

This park is really Jurassic! Well, the dinosaurs don't move, but you will find more Jurassic-age dinosaur bones, skulls, and skeletons here than anywhere else in the world. There are also weird land formations caused by the wind and rain eating away at the earth. Perfect for a dinosaur park!

Utah   Colorado

Make No Bones About It!

At this park more than 2,000 dinosaur bones are exposed on a wall inside the park building. Can you find the six dinosaurs that are hiding outside?

Utah

Bryce Canyon/Zion National Parks

Castles, people, chessmen, a box of giant stone crayons...All kinds of strange shapes can be seen in the white, purple, pink, red, orange, and yellow rocks that fill Bryce Canyon National Park. At Zion, earn a patch from the Junior Ranger program. Also check out the hanging gardens and Weeping Rock.

Rocky Road!

These two parks have beautiful and fun things to see. Find and circle them in the puzzle below.

Bike	Hike	Sun
Bryce	Lore	Top
Camp	Red	Tower
Canyon	Ride	Wall
Cliff	Rim	Zion
Fold	Rock	

E	K	C	L	I	F	F
K	C	A	M	P	O	T
I	O	N	W	A	L	L
B	R	Y	C	E	D	O
Z	I	O	N	D	E	R
S	U	N	H	I	K	E
T	O	W	E	R	I	M

Hoover Dam/Lake Mead

Nevada

Arizona

Hoover Dam is one of the highest dams in the world. Drop deep inside for a tour with a 44-story elevator ride and you still won't be at the bottom. Then, find a spot on Lake Mead to boat, fish, swim, or waterski. There's plenty of room—it's the biggest man-made lake in the United States.

Rhyme Time!
Find the rhyming answers to each pair of riddles.

It blocks a river_____
A baby sheep_____

You walk on them_____
A large red vegetable_____

A round toy_____
Great place to shop_____

They tell the time_____
Baby toys with letters_____

It has an on/off switch_____
A dog and cat may do this_____

Finger jewelry_____
Kids like to do this_____

A smile is found on this_____
Opposite of north_____

Fun to read_____
Make dinner_____

It has two wheels_____
A walk in the woods_____

Frogs like to_____
Gasoline comes out of a_____

Grand Canyon National Park

Arizona

This is one big ditch! Stand on the South Rim of the Grand Canyon, and you'll be looking a mile down and almost 10 miles across. For a different view, look up at the massive canyon walls from a raft plunging on the Colorado River. Or, ride a mule into the canyon past the colorful, layered cliffs.

Some View!

Hop aboard a mule and ride down into the Grand Canyon. See if you can find the way.

Phoenix

Want to walk through a forest of cacti? Visit the Desert Botanical Garden where mighty saguaro cacti stand at attention like prickly crossing guards. Phoenix also has a Doll and Toy Museum, the Pueblo Grande Indian Museum, and a Mystery Castle built of desert rocks.

Arizona

Prickly Place!

Deserts have beautiful cacti, wildflower, and desert plants. Color these that are found in Arizona. Saguaro's big arms have white and yellow flowers. Pink flowers crown the short, round, gray-green pincushion. Bear grass is bushy with a tall white flower. Red blossoms tip the ocotillo's long, thin branches. Prickly pear has flat, thick leaves with golden flowers. Orange blooms top the barrel cactus. Joshua tree branches have green, prickly, bushy ends. Hedgehog has dark pink blossoms.

O.K. CORRAL

Tucson/Tombstone

Arizona

Tarantulas and rattlesnakes are among the critters that hang out at the Tucson-Sonora Desert Museum—really a kind of zoo. Watch Wild West shoot-outs at Old Tucson Studios. See the graves of real Old West outlaws and lawmen on Boot Hill in nearby Tombstone. For a look at the future, stop by Biosphere 2.

Shop Till You Drop!
Shopping is always fun. Where can you find these cool souvenirs?

1

2

3

4

5

6

7

EPITAPH 8

Arizona-Sonora Desert Museum _____

Barrio Historico _____

Fort Huachuca _____

Kitt Peak Observatory _____

O.K. Corral _____

Old Tucson _____

Pima Air Museum _____

Tombstone _____

158

Santa Fe/Taos

New Mexico

Hurry over to the Museum of International Folk Art to see the huge toy display. Learn about Indians at the Museum of Indian Arts and Culture, get in on the action at the Children's Museum, or stop at the Museum of Fine Arts. Then, in Taos, visit an ancient pueblo where Indian families still live today.

Ancient Apartment House!

Taos Indians have lived here for 1,000 years, many of those years in this pueblo. Color the scene with bright cheerful colors.

Mesa Verde means "green table" in Spanish, and that's just what this huge, forest-covered rock platform looks like. But it's a table with a secret. From the top, peer down into canyons and discover ancient Indian homes built on huge shelves high in the sides of the cliff. A golden stone city waiting to be explored.

Colorado

Mesa Verde

Pick a Path!

Start up the ladder and wind your way through the ruins on one of the two paths that lead to Balcony House or follow another path to the Kiva.

KIVA

BALCONY
HOUSE

Denver/Colorado Springs

Maybe your allowance came from Denver—check out the United States Mint where lots of our coins are made. Don't just admire the mountains, climb to the top of Colorado Springs' Pikes Peak by road or cog railway, or spy on Kissing Camels in the Garden of the Gods. P.S. The skiing is great! If you like amusement parks, head for Elitch Gardens.

Colorado

Awesome!
Find the right ski trail to the bottom of Pikes Peak.

LODGE

Oklahoma City/Tulsa

Oil wells? Cowboy statues? Giant talking money? Oklahoma City has it all! Check out the Capital building, the Cowboy Hall of Fame, and Enterprise Square USA. In Tulsa, you can shop at a real Indian trading post, then head to Allen Ranch for a horseback ride, hay ride, and chuckwagon supper.

Oklahoma

Tribal Tracking!
Follow the Indian trail. Find 21 things that begin with a "t."

Did You Know?

Oklahoma has the only state capitol with oil wells on the lawn and in the basement. In Tulsa, the Gilcrease Museum, one of the world's finest Western art collections, was founded by Thomas Gilcrease, a man of Creek Indian descent who made his fortune in oil.

Dallas/Fort Worth

Cheer the bucking bronco or yell "Ride 'em cowboy!" at a real western rodeo. Investigate pioneer life at Log Cabin Village in Fort Worth or Old City Park in Dallas. The days of cattle drives come alive at the Fort Worth stockyards. For modern-day excitement, there's Six Flags Over Texas.

Texas

Catch This!
Study for one minute these items you would use to play sports. Close the book. See how many you can remember.

Explore by foot...or by boat! A river runs right through downtown. Downtown is also where you'll find that famous Spanish mission (and battle site) the Alamo, a Mexican market, and lots of great museums. When you need a history break, cheer on the watery stars at Sea World of Texas.

Buena Suerte!

San Antonio has lots of Spanish atmosphere. Identify these Spanish words from the scene below.

arbol ____   burro ____   casa ____   gato ____   iglesia ____   mano ____

niña ____   niño ____   pelo ____   pelota ____   perro ____   piñata ____

serape ____   sol ____   sombrero ____   zapatos ____

Minneapolis/St. Paul

Minnesota

Don't worry about the weather here. Glass skyways connect the downtown buildings—a hamster maze for humans! There are also lakes for swimming, fishing, and boating. Hop aboard for a sternwheeler ride on the Mississippi River. Or, explore a fort, two zoos, and an outdoor sculpture park (check out the giant cherry).

Cruisin' Down the River!

If you were Tom Sawyer or Huck Finn floating down the Mississippi River on a raft, what states would you pass on your travels?

Start at the arrow and write every other letter until you have gone around the circle twice, filling in the blanks.

M _ _ _ _ _ _ _ _

I _ _ _ _

M _ _ _ _ _ _ _

A _ _ _ _ _ _ _

L _ _ _ _ _ _ _ _

W _ _ _ _ _ _ _ _

I _ _ _ _ _ _ _

K _ _ _ _ _ _ _

T _ _ _ _ _ _ _ _

M _ _ _ _ _ _ _ _ _ _

165

Black Hills

South Dakota

This is gold country! Grab a pan and sift for nuggets like an old-time prospector, or tour a mine. Haunt a ghost town, or prowl caves filled with jewel-like crystals. Chug the tracks in an 1880 steam train. At Mt. Rushmore you'll see presidents with noses almost as long as a school bus!

Gold Mining!
Find the six hidden things about the Black Hills.

Scenic Stumpers!

How about a game to help you enjoy the scenery? Can be played with several people or alone.

1. The first player picks something from the passing scene.

2. The next person has to name something that begins with the last letter of the first item.

3. Try to stump the other players by picking something with an unusual last letter (for example "X").

4. If all are stumped by your word, you get to start the next game.

Black Hills Trivia

- Gold comes in many different colors.
- The heads on Mt. Rushmore are 60 feet from forehead to chin and took 14 years to carve.
- There are many beautiful caves to visit beneath the Black Hills.
- Bison bulls weigh nearly a ton and can run faster than a horse.
- Custer State Park has many bison and some famous begging burros.
- You can still pan for gold today in the Black Hills, in Deadwood, Lead, and Hill City.
- Wooly mammoths once lived around Hot Spings in the Black Hills.

"Wet" is the word for the Dells! Ride a duck (a special car, not a quacker) over land *and* water. Take a boat tour through narrow canyons and past weird rock formations. Pick a water park to splash and play, or watch a waterski show. Time to dry off? How about a wild round of miniature golf, or enter the future at the Tommy Bartlett Exploratory.

Wisconsin Dells

What a Wild Waterslide!
When Mary jumps in, where will she come out? Tube 1, 2, or 3?

Wisconsin

Milwaukee

Wisconsin

Walk through a rain forest or meet face-to-face with life-size dinosaurs at the Public Museum. Then, experiment with science at Discovery World. After a stop at the terrific zoo, wander through the Domes. These round plant museums are HUGE! Each is almost half a foodball field wide and seven stories tall.

Whose lunch?
Lunches got all mixed up at the zoo. Help each animal find its own lunch. Draw a line to join the right pairs.

For an eagle's-eye view of the city, soar to the top of Willis Tower—the world's tallest building. Watch whales at the Shedd Aquarium, climb through a coal mine at the Museum of Science and Industry, or enter an Egyptian tomb at the Field Museum. Then, go ape with the gorillas at Lincoln Park Zoo.

Chicago

Illinois

Great Shape!
If you try, you can see other shapes in several of the Great Lakes. Identify the lakes that have shapes like these.

LAKE SUPERIOR

MICH.

WISCONSIN

LAKE MICHIGAN

LAKE HURON

MICHIGAN

CANADA

LAKE ONTARIO

NEW YORK

LAKE ERIE

PENNSYLVANIA

ILLINOIS

INDIANA

OHIO

Did You Know?
Combine the first letters of the names of the Great Lakes to spell HOMES. It will help you remember them (Huron, Ontario, Michigan, Erie, Superior).

Dearborn

Michigan

American sights and sounds fill the Henry Ford Museum. Find cars and comics, eggbeaters and electric lights— even the chair President Lincoln was sitting in when he was shot. Next stop is the Greenfield Village, where you can visit such places as the Wright brothers' shop, Thomas Edison's laboratory, or ride on an antique carousel.

Alphabet Favorites!
Wow! Look at all of these cool things. Can you find something that begins with each letter of the alphabet.

BE MINE

Indianapolis

In the world's largest Children's Museum you can explore a cave, match wits with computers, and conduct scientific experiments. Or, "drive" a real Indy 500 car, whirl on a carousel, and zoom through deep space. Ever wanted to ride a camel? You can at the Indianapolis Zoo.

Indiana

Race Away!

You will need three different coins to play this game—two to use as markers and one to flip. Flip the coin to determine how many spaces to move—heads, move two spaces; tails move one space. Follow the directions on spaces where you land. First one to the Finish Line takes the checkered flag.

START

FINISH

LAP LEADER MOVE **3** SPACES

SPIN OUT MOVE 1 SPACE BACK

OUT OF GAS LOSE **1** TURN

NEW TIRES EXTRA TURN

PIT STOP LOSE 1 TURN

HIT THE WALL! YOU LOSE

FLAT TIRE MOVE **2** SPACES BACK

DEBRIS ON TRACK MOVE 1 SPACE BACK

CAUTION MOVE **1** SPACE

GREEN FLAG MOVE **3** SPACES

Bluegrass Country

Kentucky

Like horses? You'll LOVE Kentucky Horse Park in Lexington. There are all kinds of horsey things to see and do. For horse racing excitement, ride over to the Kentucky Derby Museum in Louisville. Or, take a sternwheeler cruise, learn "The Legend of Daniel Boone," explore a fort, or see Lincoln's birthplace.

Horses, Horses, Horses!

Can you correctly identify these parts of a horse? Fill in the numbers.

Barrel_____   Hoof_____

Chest_____   Mane_____

Fetlock_____   Nostrils_____

Forelock_____   Tail_____

Haunch_____   Thigh_____

Hock_____   Withers_____

How much do you know about horses? True or False?

A newborn horse is a foal._____

A mare is a mother horse._____

All Thoroughbred horses are one year older every January 1st. _____

Horses always sleep lying down._____

Horses were brought to America by the Spaniards. _____

The father of a horse is its sire._____

Ponies are baby horses._____

Mammoth Cave National Park

You won't find the Flintstones here, but you will find lots of other "stone age" things, such as a waterfall, icicles, needles, popcorn, snowballs, and flowers. Special sections include Fat Man's Misery, Bottomless Pit, and Mummy Ledge. Oh, don't forget a jacket—caves are really "cool" places.

Kentucky

Black Hills Trivia

Stalagmites grow up, while stalactites grow down.

Did you know that many fish in caves are either blind or have no eyes at all?

Caves are formed in limestone rocks by dripping or running water.

Mammoth Cave has more than 330 miles of explored passageways, and it is still growing.

The Snowball Dining Room is 267 feet beneath the surface.

The temperature in the cave is 54°F all year.

Mammoth Cave is the longest known cave system in the world, and there are many other caves in the area.

Bats are in some caves, but they often leave at sundown to eat.

St. Louis

Scrunch into an elevator that looks kind of like a clothes dryer, and ride up Gateway Arch to see the sights. Back on the ground, find everything from furry-footed Clydesdale horses to buffalo at Grants Farm. Catch your shadow at the Magic House, or roam the zoo and Science Center in Forest Park.

Missouri

Scrambled States!

It would be fun to visit some of these cool places, but their states are all mixed up. Unscramble the states. Then match each great place with its state.

1. SALAKA _____
2. DORFAIL _____
3. WEN KORY _____
4. FLAIRCOINA _____
5. ZORAINA _____
6. VENSILPANNAY _____
7. SCHATUMASSETS _____
8. THOUS TAKODA _____
9. REGOIGA _____
10. RISOSUMI _____
11. LISINILO _____
12. STOMENANI _____
13. SAXET _____
14. DOOLACOR _____
15. NECKTUYK _____

Alamo _____
Denali _____
Everglades _____
Golden Gate Bridge _____
Grand Canyon _____
Gateway Arch _____
Liberty Bell _____
Mammoth Cave _____
Mount Rushmore _____
Pikes Peak _____
Plymouth Rock _____
Willis Tower _____
Statue of Liberty _____
Stone Mountain _____
10,000 Lakes _____

Skinny, twisting roads roller coaster the Ozark Mountains. At the Ozark Folk Center, see what mountain life was like before there were roads. Spend a day at Silver Dollar City. Ride the rides, listen to country music, watch old-time crafters or tour a cave. Fish and swim at Table Rock Lake, or catch the shows in Branson.

Missouri

Arkansas

Ozarks

Fun Time!

Find and circle these things you can see and do on vacation. Then find the secret message in the leftover letters.

Ball	Merry-go-round
Bike	Museum
Boat	Raft
Bumper cars	Read
Camp	Ride
Cave	Roller coaster
Climb	Row
Drive	Sail
Eat	Sand castles
Ferry	Shop
Fish	Sightsee
Fly	Ski
Golf	Sled
Green	Sleep
Hike	Sports
Horse	Swim
Inner tube	Swing
Lake	Trip
Limbo	Water park
Look	Zoo

R	O	W	S	R	A	C	R	E	P	M	U	B
A	O	F	A	E	A	T	M	G	N	I	W	S
F	T	L	I	A	H	A	E	Y	L	F	E	E
T	A	O	L	D	S	T	R	O	P	S	E	L
E	O	G	R	E	E	N	R	V	I	K	S	T
Z	B	E	F	E	R	R	Y	I	I	R	T	S
A	M	U	K	I	I	C	G	B	P	A	H	A
M	I	A	T	D	S	G	O	P	O	P	G	C
U	L	O	E	R	D	H	R	A	E	R	I	D
E	C	O	L	V	E	H	O	R	S	E	S	N
S	A	A	O	L	I	N	U	P	W	T	L	A
U	V	T	M	K	A	R	N	I	I	A	E	S
M	E	M	E	P	E	B	D	I	M	W	D	R

Natchez

Clip-clop through town in a horse-drawn carriage as they did in the old days. Visit Longwood, the largest eight-sided house in the U.S., a beautiful mansion started in 1860 but never finished. Discover the life of the Natchez Indians. Along the Natchez Trace Parkway, you will find an eerie cypress swamp.

Mississippi

Shapely States!

Many states are shaped like no other state. Can you identify these states just from their shape? Check the map on pages 4 and 5, if you need a hint.

Clap to the music of street performers in the French Quarter. See the Mississippi from a sternwheeler or a ferry. Meet some "finny friends" at the aquarium, or hop on a bell-clanging streetcar to the fabulous zoo. Boat the lagoons, ride the carousel, or visit Storyland in City Park.

New Orleans

Louisiana

Sail Away!
Down the Mississippi River sail two identical sternwheelers—or are they? Can you find 10 differences between them?

Huntsville

Feeling spacey? Head for the U.S. Space and Rocket Center. You can take a bus tour of the NASA labs and shuttle test sites. Try out weightlessness, work hands-on displays, or surround yourself with an Omnimax space exploration film. An outdoor park is filled with a forest of real rockets.

Off to Space!

Rockets sprout like tulips in this rocket park. Follow-the-dots to add a few more, then color the picture.

Nashville moves to the beat of country music. Hear its sounds at Opryland USA—a park full of music shows and rides! To experience the life of the city's first settlers, visit Fort Nashborough, perched high above the Cumberland River. For outdoor fun—go boating, fishing, or hiking at Priest Lake.

Nashville
Tennessee

Music City!

Study these musical instruments for one minute.
Close the book and see how many you can remember.

Great Smoky Mountains National Park

Tennessee — North Carolina

Pull on your hiking boots and hit the trail—the Appalachian Trail. It snakes through the park high along the crest of the mountains. There are lots of shorter trails, too. See the mountain villages in the valleys hidden by bluish mist? That's the "smoke" in Great Smoky. You can camp overnight and Dollywood theme park is nearby.

Hit the Road!

The kids ran because their trip was starting. Add one letter to the letters on the first line, scramble them to form a new word. Repeat on each line. Each new word must contain all of the letters of the word above it. Hint—subtract R, A, and N from STARTING to see what letters to use.

What's in a Name?

How many words are hiding in the name
GREAT SMOKY MOUNTAINS
(100, maybe 200! No plurals, no proper names)?

Puppets from around the world hang out at the Center for Puppetry Arts. At the Cyclorama, see and hear a Civil War battle come alive as you sit inside a huge round painting. Stone Mountain is a sort of southern Mt. Rushmore. A steam train circles the mountain, plus a cable car and path climb to the top.

Atlanta

Georgia

Lots to see!

Build this pyramid with names of things to see in Atlanta. Each name must fill a complete row of squares and no more.

BRAVES

CAPITOL

CNN

CYCLORAMA

MARTA

M.L. KING SITE

OMNI

SIX FLAGS

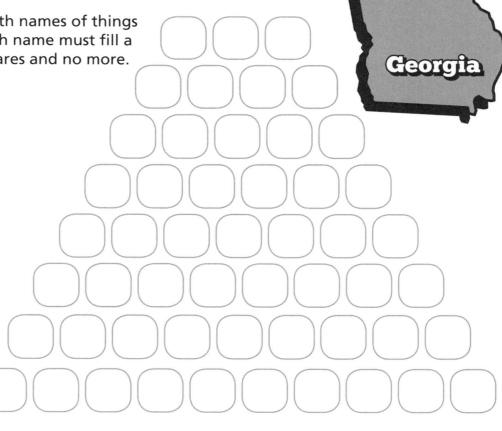

Tampa/St. Petersburg

Pack your camera and "shoot" your way through an African safari at Busch Gardens. Out on the St. Petersburg pier, you can fish, eat, or shop in an upside-down pyramid. Feel like building a sand castle or body-surfing some waves? Grab a shovel and a suit, then head for St. Pete's beaches.

Florida

Ahoy Matey!
Shiver me timbers, where's my ship? Connect the dots in order, then color the picture.

Central Florida/Orlando

Florida

This must be theme park heaven! At Walt Disney World you can meet Mickey Mouse, travel the world, or learn the stunt secrets of Indiana Jones. At Sea World, go eye-to-eye with danger as you walk through a pool of sharks. Then let Universal Studios' earthquake ride *really* shake you up.

What's Up!

What can you find in Central Florida? Solve the sentences below, then fill the right letters in the matching slots at the bottom.

1. Find me in light and toy_____
2. Find me in horse and hug_____
3. Find me in car and ride_____
4. Find me in ice and big_____
5. Find me in log and pile_____
6. Find me in line and luck_____
7. Find me in smile and sad_____

Did You Know?

Central Florida is a fun-filled playground today. Not too long ago it was mostly acres and acres of citrus groves, large cattle ranches, and a few swamps.

I spy!

If you're looking out the window, try to find something that begins with each letter of the alphabet, in order. You can play this game alone or with another traveler.

____ ____ ____ ____ ____ ____ ____
1   2   3   4   5   6   7

BOAT TOURS

ACTION

Nonstop Fun!

Unscramble these great vacation sights in central Florida.

NALROTILAGDAL _____

SPRYCES SNARGED _____

YESNID-GMM DOSITUS _____

CEPTO TENREC _____

LORDIFA RITCUS WROTE _____

ESA DORLW FO DIFROLA _____

LIVERS GRINSPS _____

KRASH COTRENUNE _____

SILVERUNA TOSSIDU RALFIDO _____

TWAL NESDIY DROWL _____

Central Florida

Want more? How about exciting waterski and bird shows at Cypress Gardens? Or Gatorland Zoo—crawling with thousands of huge and small alligators and crocodiles? Ride a glass-bottom boat over rainbow-colored fish. Find your state stone in a monument built of cement and stones from every state.

Board an airboat and skim over this "river of grass." Keep a watch out for wildlife. Birds come in many colors—red, blue, pink, white, yellow, and green. Long-legged herons stalk for fish. Alligators and crocodiles lie like floating logs. You may glimpse a shy sea cow (manatee), or see a slithery snake.

Florida

Snakes, pelicans, and gators, oh my!
Can you solve these rebus puzzles about things to see in the Everglades?

GAL. − G + 👁 + ≡ + ✕

+ 🥄 + YOU OWE $10.00

👩 − H + 🎀 + T

🪚 + 〰

C + ☁ ←

T + 👗 − SK + L

S N + 🧹 − R

Cape Canaveral/Titusville

Florida

This is where the space shuttles lift off. Start at the Kennedy Space Center to experience the blast of an imitation countdown and launch—maybe even a real one! See space capsules and space suits. And, hundreds of birds who share their sky with man.

Cape Caper!
Strange things are happening at Cape Canaveral and Merritt Island National Wildlife Refuge. Find nine things that are not quite right.

Did You Know?
Some parts of Florida have lived under as many as eight flags, since Europeans arrived in 1513.

St. Augustine

This city is OLD—the oldest in the United States. Cross the moat and climb the ramparts of a 300-year-old fort. Wander the narrow streets to find the oldest house and the oldest wooden school. Watch "Spanish settlers" at work. Stop for a sip at the Fountain of Youth or a dip at the beach.

Florida

Flag facts!
During her history, St. Augustine has lived under four flags. Can you match these flags with their countries?

1513   Spain

1763   England

1783   Spain

1821   United States of America

1861   Confederate States of America

1862   United States of America

Charleston

South Carolina

Explore a five-sided piece of American history, Fort Sumter, where the first shots of the Civil War were fired. At Magnolia Plantation, tread the boardwalks into a swamp garden. At Charles Towne Landing, see a colonial village, sailing ships, wolves, bears, pumas, and other native wildlife roaming the Animal Forest.

Spot These Sights!

Play Tic-Tac-Toe with Charleston sights. Look for the item (or something sort of like it) pictured in the square you want to play. When you find it put a coin or marker over the picture. Set a limit on how long you can look for the correct item. Each player should use a different type of coin or marker. If you are playing alone, see how long it takes you to get three in a row, or to cover the whole board.

Bridge	**Garden**	**Church**
Theater	**Fort Sumter**	**Golf Course**
Boat	**House**	**Horse and Buggy**

Cape Hatteras

North Carolina

Hit the beaches, the water's fine! Go swimming, windsurfing, or deep-sea fishing. Explore skeletons of old shipwrecks. Visit Kitty Hawk and stand on the spot where the first airplane flight took place almost 100 years ago. Try solving the mystery of the Lost Colony.

Who's Idea!

With which inventor or discoverer is each of these items linked?

Alexander Graham Bell _____

George Washington Carver _____

Pierre and Marie Curie _____

George Eastman _____

Thomas Alva Edison _____

Benjamin Franklin _____

Guglielmo Marconi _____

Samuel F.B. Morse _____

Eli Whitney _____

Orville and Wilbur Wright _____

Williamsburg

Virginia

A peacock parades across a green common. In the shops, wigs are sewn, barrels are shaped, and teapots are carefully crafted out of fine silver. A wooden stock waits to trap those who misbehave. Men in frock coats visit with women in hoop-skirted dresses. Welcome to Colonial Williamsburg!

You Make What?

Match the historic names of these tradesmen with the items they made. Fill in the proper number after its matching trade.

Apothecary—————

Baker—————

Blacksmith—————

Cabinetmaker—————

Chemist—————

Cooper—————

Milliner—————

Peruke Maker—————

Silversmith—————

Wheelwright—————

4

1

2

3

9

5

6

7

8

On Jamestown Island, park of Colonial National Historical Park, see the ruins of the first permanent English settlement in America. Nearby, stop at the glass house where melted blobs of glass are blown into bowls and vases. Also, see replicas of the ships on which the settlers arrived. At nearby Yorktown, visit a Revolutionary War battlefield.

Jamestown

Virginia

Colorful History!
Color by number:
1. Brown   2. Black
3. Green   4. Yellow
5. Red   6. Light blue   7. Orange

Baltimore

Rustle through a rain forest, stare down a shark, beware of the red-bellied piranha when you enter the National Aquarium. Climb aboard a ship that battled pirates almost 200 years ago. Visit Babe Ruth's birthplace and Ft. McHenry—the site of the battle that inspired the "Star Spangled Banner."

Fancy Fins!

See all of the beautiful fish. Only two of them are alike. Can you find them?

Washington, D.C.

Maryland

Visit with pandas, or stop in at the president's house. Climb down the Washington Monument. Watch the FBI in action. Cruise a canal in a mule-drawn boat. In the museums, find Dorothy's ruby slippers, Teddy Roosevelt's teddy bear, a moon rock to touch, the Wright Brother's plane, and live bugs to play with.

Oh Say Can You See in Washington, D.C.?
Fill in the sights.

Museums: Freer

Smithsonian

U.S. Holocaust

Memorials: Jefferson

Lincoln

Vietnam Veterans

(The) Wall

Capitol

Congress

FBI

Ford's Theater

Kennedy Center

Mall

Potomac (River)

Supreme Court

Union (Station)

Washington Monument

White House

Wolf Trap

Zoo

Capital Quiz!

How much do you know about our nation's capital? Try this quiz and see.

What is the tallest masonry (stone or brick) structure in the world?

Where do they print money?

What monument has 58,156 names on it?

Where can you find the Wright Brothers' 1903 *Flyer*, Lindbergh's *Spirit of St. Louis*,
  and the *Apollo* command module?

Where does the president live?

What is found on the land surrounding
Robert E. Lee's former home?

What is the "Castle?"

Where can you find a dragon?

Where can you see a panda?

What two letters in American Sign Language do
  Lincoln's hands form on his statue at the Lincoln Memorial?

Pittsburgh

Pennsylvania

Downtown sits in a "Golden Triangle." Rivers sweep by two sides to form the Ohio River at the triangle's point. Creep steeply up Mount Washington by incline (hill-climbing trolleys) for a great view of all three rivers. Control your own sky trip at the Science Center. Roam Dinosaur Hall at the Natural History Museum.

Solve the Mystery!

How many triangles are hidden in this mysterious pyramid? How many can you find?

Secret clue...some are made up of more than one little triangle!

Did You Know?

Once dark and dingy from steel mills and mines, today Pittsburgh is a beautiful modern city. It has shining steel and glass buildings, lots of museums, music, and sports.

Lancaster

Pennsylvania

Enter the world of the Amish. Children study in one-room schools. Men have beards and women wear bonnets. See mule-drawn plows and horse-drawn buggies (even ride in one), but no electric lights—or TV! Nearby Hershey has chocolate air, kiss-shaped streetlights, and a fascinating theme park.

Plain or Fancy?

Many Amish people often do not use modern or fancy things. Draw a line to those they would use. Which would they not use?

Philadelphia

Pennsylvania

This is where America was born. Visit Independence Hall and see the Liberty Bell. At Penn's Landing, board a battleship or squeeze into a submarine. The world's largest "pinball machine" and lots of super science stuff is in the Franklin Institute. America's first zoo has a four-story treehouse to climb!

Did You Know?

Philly is famous for...
The Liberty Bell (a must-see for everyone)
Hot pretzels (with or without mustard) sold by corner vendors
Cheese steak sandwiches (a tasty treat)

Did You Know That?

Philadelphia was the home of many famous firsts.

The first U.S. flag, with 13 stars and 13 stripes, was made in Philadelphia. Tradition says, by Betsy Ross.

The first U.S. zoo (1874)

The first Bank of the United States (1797)

The first stock exchange (1790)

The first fire-fighting company (1776)

The first U.S. mint to coin money (1792)

The first daily newspaper (1784)

The first bifocal glasses, invented by Ben Franklin

The first public library (1731)

The first root beer, invented by Charles Hires (1866)

The first ice cream soda (1861)

The first motion picture show in the world (1870)

The first public demonstration of the telephone (1876)

Can You Come Out Even?

As you follow around the square, add and subtract, as directed, the number related to each item listed in the little squares. See if you can come out with the same totals as given at two of the corners.

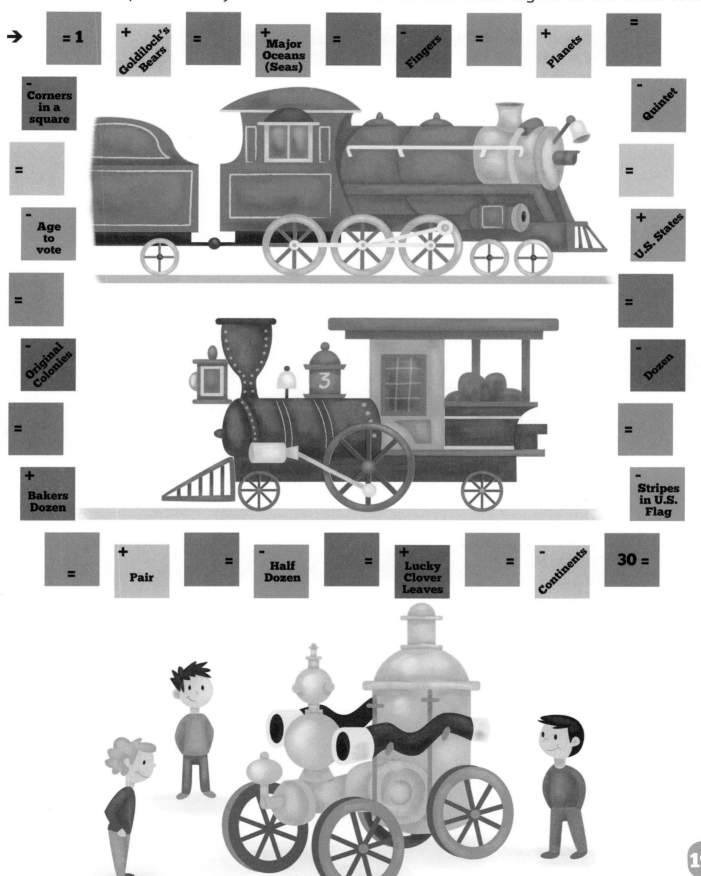

→ = 1   + Goldilock's Bears   = + Major Oceans (Seas)   = − Fingers   = + Planets   =

− Corners in a square

− Quintet

=

=

− Age to vote

+ U.S. States

=

=

− Original Colonies

− Dozen

=

=

+ Bakers Dozen

− Stripes in U.S. Flag

=   + Pair   =   − Half Dozen   =   + Lucky Clover Leaves   =   − Continents   30 =

Valley Forge

Pennsylvania

Gaze out over the beautiful rolling green hills of this national historical park, and try to imagine you're a soldier in the winter of 1777. It is arctic cold. You're hungry and sick. The tiny log hut you share with other soldiers is bare and dark. General Washington makes battle plans in the stone house that is his headquarters. Life was hard at Valley Forge.

Silent Sentinels!
Antique cannons sit silently, reminding us of the hard-fought American Revolution, when we won our freedom. Two are alike. Find them.

Niagara Falls

These falls are part American and part Canadian. Peer down on them from a tower almost 300 feet high. For a closer view, head for the island at the edge of the plunging water. For a REALLY close look (you'll get wet) take a boat ride past the base of the falls, or walk right into the spray.

New York

Awesome!
Guide *The Maid of the Mist* safely through the thundering waters back to the pier.

The Statue of Liberty and Brooklyn Bridge are only a couple of the famous landmarks in America's largest city. Chug past the sights on a ferry. Buy a hot dog from a street-corner cart. Don't miss the zoo and carousel in Central Park, the Natural History Museum and the Sea, Air & Space Museum, or the ships at South Street Seaport.

New York

New York

Did You Know?
More than 17 million immigrants (90% of the total) entered the United States through Ellis Island between 1892 and 1954. The one-day record was 12,000 on April 17, 1907. Today Ellis Island is part of the Statue of Liberty National Monument.

Build Your Own Skyscraper!
How many blocks are in this stack? There are no hidden spaces. Sort of looks like a skyscraper, doesn't it?

CIRCLE LINE

Mystic

Tall masts creak and sway as ships ride at anchor in an 1800s fishing village. Scramble over the decks of a whaling ship and a square-rigger. Help set a ship's sails. Listen to hammers pound as you watch ships being built. Make rope and learn to tie knots like a sailor. Stop by the nearby aquarium.

Connecticut

Ship Ahoy!

Let's color this Mystic Seaport scene. Follow the numbers.

1. Green   2. Yellow   3. Brown   4. Light blue   5. Blue
6. Gray   7. Purple   8. Black   9. Red

Climb sand dunes and race small shore birds along the beaches. Swim, boat, go fishing, or go whale watching. See an Aqua Circus. Climb Pilgrim Monument tower. Like to bike? There are great bike trails all over Cape Cod. Or, ferry out to Martha's Vineyard or Nantucket for two-wheel island exploring.

Cape Cod
Massachusetts

Chart Challenge!

Match the names of these geographic features with their numbers on the map.

Bay _____   Lake _____

Canal _____   Ocean _____

Cape _____   Peninsula _____

Channel _____   Reservoir _____

Dam _____   River _____

Delta _____   Sound _____

Inlet _____   Tributary _____

Island _____

Plymouth

Massachusetts

See Plymouth Rock where the Pilgrims landed in 1620, and explore the small, crowded quarters of a replica of their ship, the *Mayflower.* At Plimoth Plantation, the Pilgrims will take time to chat with you as they go about their daily chores—cooking, mending a roof, gardening, or tending the livestock.

Decode It!
Crack the code to solve these Plymouth sights.

A = ◆   N = ✿
B = ✳   O = ↑
C = ✓   P = ▼
D = △   Q = ☽
E = ◇   R = ☆
F = ✕   S = □
G = ■   T = ▲
H = ○   U = ↓
I = ✴   V = ❖
J = ●   W = ✧
K = ✚   X = ✦
L = ▽   Y = →
M = ⌘   Z = ←

▼▽✳⌘↑▲○   ▼▽◆✿▲◆▲✳↑✿
_____

⌘◆→✕▽↑✧◇☆
_____

▼▽→⌘↑↓▲○   ✿↑✓✚
_____

▼✳▽■☆✳⌘   ❖✳▽▽◆■◇
_____

✕↑☆◇✕◆▲○◇☆□   ⌘↑✿↓⌘◇✿▲
_____

⌘→▽◇□   □▲◆✿△✳□○   ⌘↑✿↓⌘◇✿▲
_____

▼✳▽■☆✳⌘   ○◆▽▽   ⌘↓□◇↓⌘
_____

↑▽△   ✕↑☆▲   ○↑↓□◇
_____

205

Look down, find the red marks...then walk your way through history. Peek into Paul Revere's house, visit John Hancock's grave, tread the decks of "Old Ironsides." Go modern at a hands-on Computer Museum. Visit the four-story aquarium, ride a swan boat, or eat at the Quincy Market food stalls.

Boston
Massachusetts

Follow the Freedom Trail!

The green brick line leads to history. The trail is 3 miles long. Here are the highlights.

1 Begin at Boston Common–
Oldest U.S. public park

2 State House and Archives (1795)

3 Park Street Church (1809)
Gun powder factory, War of 1812

4 Granary Burying Ground
John Hancock, Samuel Adams, and Paul Revere are buried here

5 King's Chapel (1754)

6 First Public School Site (1635)
and Benjamin Franklin statue

7 Old Corner Bookstore (1712)
Famous authors met here

8 Old South Meeting House (1729)
Boston Tea Party began here

9 Old State House (1713)
Now Museum of Boston History

10 Boston Massacre Site
British soldiers fought colonists

11 Faneuil Hall (1742)
Called "the Cradle of Liberty"

12 Paul Revere House (ca. 1680)
Oldest Structure in Boston

13 Old North Church-Christ Church (1723)
City's oldest church still in use. In April 1775, lanterns in the steeple warned of the British coming—one if by land; two if by sea

14 Copp's Hill Burial Ground (1660)

15 U.S.S. Constitution ("Old Ironsides")
Oldest commissioned U.S. warship afloat; also museum

16 Bunker Hill Monument
Battle on June 17, 1775

U.S.S. Constitution

Boston Harbor

Old State House

Bunker Hill Monument

Acadia National Park

Acadia National Park, located mostly on an island, is full of the sounds and sights of the sea. Salty waves crash against tumbled, rocky cliffs and boom into Thunder Hole. Whales slide by, and lobster boats haul in the day's catch. Sailboats dart with the wind. Climb 1,530-foot Cadillac Mountain. Take a cold ocean swim.

Maine

Rocky Hideaway!
Find six secret objects along the rugged coast of Maine.

kids' road atlas

Using an Atlas
Pages 4-5
Everglades; Florida; Denver; Colorado; Newport Beach; California; Tijuana
The adventure begins with a turn of the page!

United States
Page 7
1. AL; 2. AK; 3. AZ; 4. AR; 5. CA; 6. CO; 7. CT; 8. DE; 9. FL; 10. GA; 11. HI; 12. ID; 13. IL; 14. IN; 15. IA; 16. KS; 17. KY; 18. LA; 19. ME; 20. MD; 21. MA; 22. MI; 23. MN; 24. MS; 25. MO; 26. MT; 27. NE; 28. NV; 29. NH; 30. NJ; 31. NM; 32. NY; 33. NC; 34. ND; 35. OH; 36. OK; 37. OR; 38. PA; 39. RI; 40. SC; 41. SD; 42. TN; 43. TX; 44. UT; 45. VT; 46. VA; 47. WA; 48. WV; 49. WI; 50. WY

Alabama
Page 8
Huntsville, Alabama

Alaska
Page 9

Arizona
Page 10
How deep?
$40 \div 10 = 4$ Empire State Buildings (up to 5,500 feet deep)
How long?
$191+60-10+17+19=277$ miles long (Utah is 270 miles wide)

Arkansas
Page 11 (clockwise from top left)
Fort Smith; Little Rock; Pine Bluff; El Dorado, Texarkana

California
Page 13
1. Redding; 2. Sequoia; 3. Joshua Tree; 4. Yosemite; 5. Kings Canyon; 6. Death Valley
State motto: "Eureka!"

Colorado
Page 14
B-5 Boulder; C-3 Rifle; A-3 Steamboat Springs; B-6 Brush; A-2 Dinosaur National Monument; A-6 Crow River; C-5 Castle Rock

Connecticut
Page 15 (Penguins)

Delaware
Page 16

208 Answers

Florida
Page 17

OCEAN and CANOE; PALM and LAMP; PEARS and SPEAR; MELON and LEMON; TEN and NET; SHOE and HOSE; BEARD and BREAD

Georgia
Page 18

Hawaii
Page 19

Kilauea is an active volcano in Hawaii Volcanoes National Park.

Idaho
Page 20

Illinois
Page 21

1. Paris; 2. Beardstown;
3. Sandwich; 4. Rock Falls;
5. Normal; 6. Champaign

Indiana
Page 22

1st – #2 orange; 2nd – #10 red; 3rd – #8 yellow

Iowa
Page 24

1. PIG
2. ROOSTER
3. SHEEP
4. COW
5. GOAT
6. HORSE
7. CHICKEN

More popcorn is produced in Sioux City, Iowa, than in any other place in the world.

Kansas
Page 25

Kentucky
Page 26

(B-4) Louisville; (B-5) Frankfort and Lawrenceburg;
(B-6) Lexington; (C-3) Owensboro; (C-5) Danville;
(C-6) Richmond; (C-8) Pikeville; (D-3) Russellville;
(D-4) Bowling Green; (D-6) London & Williamsburg

Louisiana
Page 27

Maine
Page 28

Maryland
Page 29

He was a prisoner on a British ship.

Massachusetts
Page 31

Michigan
Page 32

Standard

Minnesota
Page 33

Across: 3. Mille; 4. Vermilion; 6. Leech
Down: 1. Upper Red; 2. Winnibigoshish; 5. L. Itasca;
6. Lower Red

Mississippi
Page 34

paddlewheel, paddle, pail, palm tree, pants,
park, park bench, parking meter, parrot, patch
(eye), path, paw, pegleg, pelican, pencil, pepper,
periscope, person, picnic, pier, pig, pillow,
pineapple, pipe, pirate, plane, plate, pony, poodle,
post, puddle

Missouri
Page 35

Montana
Page 36

Nebraska
Page 37

Nevada
Page 38

Las Vegas

New Hampshire
Page 39

ship, ramp, shrimp, man, pines, pear, pie, peas, sheep

New Jersey
Page 40

New Mexico
Page 41

New York
Page 42-43

mail box, periscope, sailboat on rock, snow boarder, candy cane, chimney on tent, fishing in fire, fire hydrant, dolphin in stream, shoe in tree

North Carolina
Page 44

frog, flashlight, fish, fin (on fish), flamingo, feather, fire or flame, fruit, flower, farmer, fan, flag, flippers, football, fork, foot/feet, face, forehead, fingers, fringe (on towel or blanket), frisbee, four (on flag), fence, funnel, floats, frankfurter

North Dakota
Page 45

1. Bowman; 2. Grand Forks; 3. Valley City; 4. Rugby; 5. Devil's Lake; 6. Carrington

Ohio
Page 47

Findlay, Newark, Ashland, Canton, Whitehall, Springfield, Logan, Athens, Portsmouth, Oxford, Fairborn, Middletown

Oklahoma
Page 48

dine — Enid (B–5); bilead — Idabel (E–8); lowtan — Lawton (E–5); wlassail — Sallisaw (C–8); leekomug — Okmulgee (C–7) ; moungy — Guymon (A–2); usalt — Tulsa (B–7); amimi — Miami (A–8); sheenwa — Shawnee (C–6); talliwerts — Stillwater (B–6)

Oregon
Page 49

Pennsylvania
Page 50

Rhode Island
Page 51

1. red light; 2. redwood; 3. red, white, and blue; 4. see red; 5. Little Red Riding Hood; 6. red carpet; 7. redhead

South Carolina
Page 52

South Dakota
Page 53

The correct order is P, E, O, P, L, E, which spells out PEOPLE

Tennessee
Page 54

Texas
Page 57

Utah
Page 58

```
T G R P P H B L S T I Y T
T L I N E S A R C H E S C
A E B A O R E Z Q R O M H
Z N N T P D I N O S A U R
R C O U L E N N B K I R I
O A O R E F G S G N T A S
L N T A O E X D O Z B D Q
N Y F L F G G I L L I B K
G O G B E C W N D A W O F
L N K R A P S H E C V Y N
A S T I R D O U N H R R D
D D A D T E N D S B O C R
E T E G H V P L P A I H A
N X R E O Y T S I M I S I
S O R S K B R A K N S O V
C A P I T O L R E E F G S
M G I L K B I I J R I O O
A Q R L E B S H O A O N G
O J C R A Y A D C L N A H
C A N Y O N L A N D S P C
T A H H R N I M L A W M I
R C A L E X S Y T L P I N
S K A E R B R A D E C T C
```

Vermont
Page 59

A = 7; B = 3; C = 1; X = 5
Fact number 5 is false.

Virginia
Page 60

Williamsburg

Washington
Page 62

Father's Day.

West Virginia
Page 63

1. Weirton; 2. Ohio; 3. Weston; 4. Potomac;
5. Harpers Ferry; 6. Tug Fork; 7. Kentucky;
8. Charleston
Fact: The New River is America's oldest river.

Wisconsin
Page 64

1. B; 2. A; 3. R; 4. A; 5. B; 6. O; 7. O (Baraboo)

Wyoming
Page 65

Canada
Page 67

Mexico
Page 68-69

1. Caribbean Sea; 2. Tijuana; 3. Tabasco;
4. Tortilla; 5. Rio Grande; 6. Acapulco; 7. Mexicali;
8. Chihuahua; 9. Pacific Ocean; 10. Guatemala;
11. Ciudad Juárez; 12. El Paso; 13. Belize;
14. Hermosillo
"Mexicans were once known as the men of corn."

are we there yet?

Page 73

Page 74

1. C; 2. A; 3. H; 4. F; 5. B;
6. D; 7. E; 8. G; 9. I

Page 75

Page 76

Drop some crumbs
for us!

Page 82

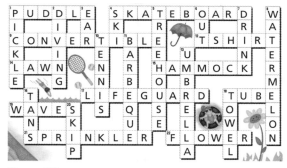

Page 83

table, tablecloth, tackle box, tag, tape, taxi, teapot,
teddy bear, teeth, telephone, ten (on a price tag),
tennis racket, tent, thermometer, thermos, thumb,
ticket, tie, tools, toothbrush, towel, toys, trees, tricycle,
trunk, T-shirt, Tuesday (on calendar), turtleneck,
tuxedo, and typewriter

Page 84

1. B; 2. J; 3. D; 4. K; 5. M; 6. F; 7. G; 8. O; 9. C; 10. A;
11. H; 12. E; 13. I; 14. L; 15. N

Page 77

Page 85

1. steering wheel; 2. hood; 3. accelerator; 4. trunk;
5. windshield; 6. brake; 7. dashboard; 8. wheel;
9. gearshift; 10. engine; 11. headlight; 12. bumper;
13. muffler; 14. battery

Page 86

Page 87

1. beach umbrella is inside out; 2. lifeguard is facing the
wrong way; 3. man in water is dressed in evening wear;
4. fisherman is fishing with a rake; 5. skiier is skiing
without a boat; 6. people warming up at a campfire;
7. golfer on the beach; 8. people playing volleyball
with a football; 9. sailboat has an upside-down sail;
10. in-line skater on the sand

Page 89

1. park hours on sign are only at night; 2. missing
rungs on slide ladder; 3. alligator in the fountain;
4. pterodactyl in the sky; 5. inner tube slide spills out
onto a golf tee; 6. big pair of glasses on the inner tube
slide ramp; 7. queen in the lifeguard chair; 8. ice skater
skating on the pool; 9. bed in the pool; 10. playing card
lying on the deck; 11. herd of sheep in the picnic area.

Page 90

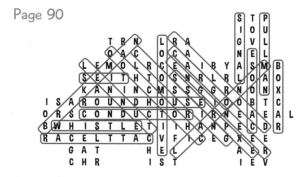

Page 91

1. buttercup; 2. pansy; 3. snapdragon; 4. carnation;
5. foxglove; 6. daisy; 7. cowslip; 8. goldenrod

Page 92

Michelle trail 1, Juan trail 2, and Keisha trail 3.

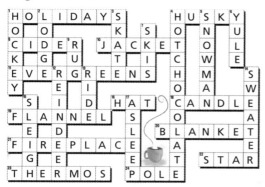

The man in the convertible wasn't telling the truth because he couldn't have driven from Salt Lake City in Utah to Chattanooga in Tennessee in 12 hours.

Say this three times fast: She sells seashells by the seashore.

1. dog; 2. cat; 3. cow; 4. toad; 5. duck; 6. goat; 7. crow; 8. goose; 9. mouse; 10. horse; 11. robin; 12. rabbit; 13. raccoon; 14. squirrel

1. F; 2. G; 3. E; 4. D; 5. H; 6. A; 7. I; 8. C; 9. B; 10. J

1. large bike's seat is backwards; 2. yield sign is upside-down; 3. spokes missing on small bike; 4. center line on road is weaving; 5. tree growing in middle of road; 6. zebra; 7. airplane flying upside-down; 8. sun in front of cloud; 9. cow in distance is as big as the house; 10. no straps on backpack

1. You can buy a necklace, polished rock, postcard, wind-up toy, and candy for exactly 205 tickets.
2. Or, you can buy a key ring, candy, giant pencil, and postcard for exactly 205 tickets.

The Sleep Inn is the correct hotel.

Page 110

Page 115

1. peanut butter and jelly; 2. taco; 3. macaroni and cheese; 4. spaghetti; 5. hamburger

Page 116

1. ark; 2. ship; 3. raft; 4. canoe; 5. yacht; 6. kayak;
7. barge 8. tugboat; 9. gondola; 10. sailboat;
11. submarine; 12. windsurfer; 13. aircraft carrier

Page 117

Page 118

Page 119

The lady couldn't have a son. She explained that she only had a sister. That sister's father (her father) had a wife (her mother) whose mother (her grandmother) had a great granddaughter (her daughter, since her sister has no children) who has a twin sister (also her daughter) who has no brother. If her daughters have no brother, she couldn't have a son. Also, North Carolina isn't the Peach State, Georgia is.

Page 121

Skiiers B and H are exactly alike.

Page 122

Page 123

Page 124

Page 125

How does a country vote for a new symbol? They have a flag poll.

Page 132

1. Picture Park 2. Travel Time; 3. Wacky water park;
4. You're bugging ME!; 5. On the Right Track;
6. Bloomers; 7. Happy Camper?; 8. Barnyard SCRAMBLE;
9. Travel Journal

Are you there yet?

coast-to-coast games

Page 138

Cinder cone	5	Lava	3
Crater	1	Magma	2
Eruption	6	Vent	8
Gas and ash	7	Volcanic bombs	4

Page 139

Page 142

Black bear	Antelope
Geysers	Bighorn sheep
Bison	Yellowstone Falls
Mammoth Hot Springs	Bald Eagle
Grizzly bear	Old Faithful
Moose	Paint Pots
Elk (Wapiti)	Beaver

Page 143

Stream	Bread
Table	Bed
Potato	Violin, guitar
Garden	Macaroni, sink pipe
Chair	Cypress tree
Clock	Corn
Wristwatch	Gloves
River	

Page 144

Gum wrapper	1 month
Orange peel	3 months
Pop can	200-500 years
Styrofoam cup	Over 500 years
Rubber tire	Over 500 years
Plastic pop rings	Over 500 years
Glass bottle	1,000,000 years

Page 145

```
            G O L F
 I C E S K A T E
            S K I
        R I D E
            T E N N I S
        S A I L
        H I K E
        B O A T
  W A T E R S K I
```

Page 146

12 states

New York	Indiana	Wyoming
New Jersey	Illinois	Utah
Pennsylvania	Iowa	Nevada
Ohio	Nebraska	California

Page 147

```
          C      A H W A H N E E
 M E A D O W        A
 E     N        S L     E
 R N Y O S E M I T E F A L L S
 C O   E        E D     C
 F E R N Q      R O   P A S S
 D   U      R O A M   P
     C O    A   E   H I K E
 M A R I P O S A       T   D
     M A        L   A   Y
     P          M O U N T A I N   T
 T R A I L      K       I   H
 O   N   T U O L U M N E   V A L E
 C   G   R      U       I   A
 K       R E A G L E   T   P E A K
         E              W     E
```

Page 148

CARAMEL	CAROUSEL
CARAWAY	CARPENTER
CARBURETOR	CARPET
CARDS	CARRIAGE
CARDINAL	CARROT
CAREFUL	CARTON
CARNIVAL	

Page 149

Disneyland
Knott's Berry Farm
Hollywood
Farmer's Market
Sea World
Rancho La Brea Tar Pits
Hollywood Bowl
Six Flags Magic Mountain
Universal Studios Hollywood
Queen Mary
Beverly Hills
Rose Bowl
Gene Autry Western Heritage Museum
NBC Studios
Griffith Park Observatory
The Coliseum

Page 150

The middle section in the left column matches the bottom section in the right column.

Ages of trees:

8	10
11	6
7	11

Page 151

Giraffe	Lion	Kangaroo
Elephant	Zebra	Hippopotamus
Cheetah	Monkey	

Page 152

1. Indianapolis, Oklahoma City
2. Annapolis, Maryland
3. Baton Rouge, Louisiana
4. Lincoln, Nebraska
5. Nashville, Tennessee
6. Dover, Delaware; Honolulu,

Hawaii; Indianapolis, Indiana; Oklahoma City, Oklahoma

7. Juneau, Alaska (Honolulu, Hawaii can be reached by car from other parts of Oahu Island)

8. Sacramento, California; Saint Paul, Minnesota; Salem, Oregon; Salt Lake City, Utah; Santa Fe, New Mexico; Springfield, Illinois

9. Santa Fe, New Mexico; established in 1610

10. Pierre (South Dakota)

Page 153

Page 154

Page 155

Dam	Ring
Lamb	Sing or Swing
Feet	Mouth
Beet	South
Ball	Book
Mall	Cook
Clocks	Bike
Blocks	Hike
Light	Jump
Fight	Pump

Page 156

Page 157

Saguaro
Ocotillo
Joshua tree
Barrel
Pincushion
Hedgehog
Bear grass
Prickly pear

Page 158

Arizona-Sonora Desert Museum	5
Barrio Historico	7
Fort Huachuca	4
Kitt Peak Observatory	1
O.K. Corral	3
Old Tucson	6
Pima Air Museum	2
Tombstone	8

Page 160

(maze image with labels KIVA, BALCONY HOUSE)

Page 162

Trees	Triangle (fire)	Totem
TeePee	Tribesman	Tumbleweed
Tentpoles	Torch	Thistle
Tear	Teeth	Tongue
Toad	Thumb	Tail
Tracks	Tomahawk	Travois
Tom-tom	Toe	Turtle

Page 164

arbol	10	tree
burro	6	donkey
casa	1	house
gato	5	cat
iglesia	3	church, mission
mano	13	hand
niña	12	girl
niño	15	boy
pelo	11	hair
pelota	14	ball
perro	4	dog
piñata	9	candy-filled toy
serape	8	shawl
sol	2	sun
sombrero	7	hat
zapatos	16	shoes

Page 165

Minnesota	Wisconsin
Iowa	Illinois
Missouri	Kentucky
Arkansas	Tennessee
Louisiana	Mississippi

Page 166

Pan	Pickaxe	Shovel
Burro	Miner	Bag of gold

Page 168

Tube 2

Page 169

Bird	Worm
Dog	Bone
Rabbit	Carrot
Bear	Fish
Otter	Shellfish
Giraffe	Leaves
Ape	Banana
Elephant	Peanuts

Page 170

Man with a pack	Lake Huron
Cucumber	Lake Michigan
Wolf head	Lake Superior

Page 171

A	Apple	N	Necklace
B	Ball	O	Orange
C	Candy (sucker)	P	Pail (and shovel)
D	Doll	Q	Quoits
E	Elephant	R	Race car
F	Flashlight	S	Sled
G	Goldfish	T	Tom-tom
H	Hobbyhorse	U	Unicycle
I	Ice cream	V	Valentine
J	Jet (airplane)	W	Wristwatch
K	Keys	X	Xylophone
L	Locomotive	Y	Yo-yo
M	Mitt	Z	Zebra

Page 173

Parts of a horse:

Barrel	7
Chest	10
Fetlock	8
Forelock	12
Haunch	3
Hock	5
Hoof	9
Mane	1
Nostrils	11
Tail	4
Thigh	6
Withers	2

True or false:

T   F   T   F   T   T   F

Page 175

1.	Alaska	13	Alamo
2.	Florida	1	Denali
3.	New York	2	Everglades
4.	California	4	Golden Gate Bridge
5.	Arizona	5	Grand Canyon
6.	Pennsylvania	10	Gateway Arch
7.	Massachusetts	6	Liberty Bell
8.	South Dakota	15	Mammoth Cave
9.	Georgia	8	Mount Rushmore
10.	Missouri	14	Pikes Peak
11.	Illinois	7	Plymouth Rock
12.	Minnesota	11	Willis Tower
13.	Texas	3	Statue of Liberty
14.	Colorado	9	Stone Mountain
15.	Kentucky	12	10,000 Lakes

Page 176

Message: Have a good time

Page 177

Left to right:
Top row — Idaho, Nebraska, Illinois, West Virginia, New Hampshire
Row 2 — California, Texas, Mississippi, Florida

Page 178

Paddlewheel
Flag on prow
Smokestack
Flag on pilot house
First deck 3rd window from right
Second deck near window
Second deck railing
Windows on pilot house
Color of flag on stern

Page 181

These are two possible answers:

RAN	RAN
RAIN	RANG
TRAIN	GRANT
STRAIN	GRANTS
STARING	RATINGS
STARTING	STARTING

Page 182

CNN
OMNI
MARTA
BRAVES
CAPITOL
SIX FLAGS
CYCLORAMA
M.L. KING SITE

Page 184

THRILLS

Page 185

Alligatorland
Cypress Gardens
Disney-MGM Studios
Epcot Center
Florida Citrus Tower
Sea World of Florida
Silver Springs
Shark Encounter
Universal Studios Florida
Walt Disney World

Page 186

Alligators
Spoonbill
Airboat
Sawgrass
Crane
Turtle
Snake

Page 187

Upside down:
Pelican
Rocket
Space Shuttle
Turtle
Swimming duck

Astronaut on outside of rocket
Heron sitting on rocket
Fish swimming on land
Cattails growing on bottom of stems

Page 188

Flags:
Top row: United States, Confederate States of America
Bottom row: England, Spain

Page 190

Alexander Graham Bell Telephone	5
George Washington Carver Peanut products	2
Pierre and Marie Curie Radium	8
George Eastman Roll film for cameras	10
Thomas Alva Edison Electric lights	1

Benjamin Franklin   4
   Electricity
Guglielmo Marconi   9
   Radio
Samuel F.B. Morse   6
   Telegraph, Morse Code
Eli Whitney   7
   Cotton gin
Orville and Wilbur Wright   3
   Airplane (sustained flight)

Page 191

Apothecary	7	Medicine
Baker	4	Pie
Blacksmith	2	Horseshoe
Cabinetmaker	9	Chair
Chemist	7	Medicine
Cooper	3	Barrel
Milliner	6	Hat, bonnet
Peruke maker	5	Wig
Silversmith	8	Candlestick
Wheelwright	1	Wheel

Page 193

Page 194

```
      C        W O L F T R A P
  M A L L      A
    P          S     K       F B I
U   I          H     E   Z O O     J
S M I T H S O N I A N     R     D   E
H   O          N     S    D     S   F
O   L   C O N G R E S S   U     T   F
L   T          T     D    P     H   E
O   W A L L    O     Y    P     E   R
C   H   I      N     C    R     A   S
A   V I E T N A M V E T E R A N S   O
U   T   C      O     N    M     T   N
S   E   O      N     T    E     E
T   H   L      U     E    C     R
    O   N      M     R    O
    U          E          R
    S          N        U N I O N
F R E E R      T        P O T O M A C
```

Page 195

Washington Monument
Bureau of Engraving and Printing
Vietnam Veterans' Memorial
National Air & Space Museum
The White House
Arlington National Cemetery
Smithsonian Institution (main building)
Chinatown
National Zoological Park
A and L

Page 196

40 triangles

Page 197

Would use:
   candle
   plain coat and hat
   mule and plow
   buggy
   button
   plain dress
Would not use:
   Automobile
   Zipper
   Electricity
   Electric lamp
   Telephone
   Camera

Page 199

3	bears
7	oceans
10	fingers
9	planets
5	quintet
50	U.S. states
12	dozen
13	flag stripes
7	continents
4	lucky clover leaves
6	half dozen
2	pair
13	baker's dozen
13	original colonies
18	age to vote
4	corners in a square

Page 200

The second and fourth cannons from the left match

Page 201

Page 202

27 blocks

Page 204

Bay	11
Canal	10
Cape	13
Channel	2
Dam	4
Delta	7
Inlet	9
Island	15
Lake	8
Ocean	12
Peninsula	3
Reservoir	1
River	5
Sound	14
Tributary	6

Page 205

Plimoth Plantation
Mayflower
Plymouth Rock
Pilgrim Village
Forefathers' Monument
Myles Standish Monument
Pilgrim Hall Museum
Old Fort House

Page 207

Canoe on the shore
Sailboat in the clouds
Moose head in the water
Lobster, fish, and clam in the rocks

Populations are from the 2010 U.S. Census or other national censuses.